FIRST PAST THE POST

Non-Verbal Reasoning:

2D

Multiple Choice

Book 1

© 2018 ElevenPlusExams.co.uk   COPYING STRICTLY PROHIBITED

How to use this book to make the most of 11 plus exam preparation

It is important to remember that for 11 plus exams there is no national syllabus, no pass mark and no retake option. It is therefore vital that your child is fully primed to perform to the best of their ability so that they give themselves the best possible chance on the day.

Non-Verbal Reasoning: 2D

This topic-based workbook is representative of the question styles included in the standard non-verbal reasoning section of contemporary multi-discipline 11 plus tests, which typically have two papers containing around a dozen questions each.

The suggested time for each test is based on data obtained from classroom-testing sessions held at our centre.

Never has it been more useful to learn from mistakes!

Students can improve by as much as 15%, not only by focused practice, but also by targeting any weak areas.

How to manage your child's practice

To get the most up-to-date information, visit our website, www.elevenplusexams.co.uk, the UK's largest online resource for 11 plus, with over 65,000 webpages and a forum administered by a select group of experienced moderators.

About the authors

The Eleven Plus Exams' **First Past The Post®** series has been created by a team of experienced tutors and authors from leading British universities.

Published by Technical One Ltd t/a Eleven Plus Exams

With special thanks to all the children who tested our material at the ElevenPlusExams centre in Harrow.

ISBN: 978-1-912364-87-9

Copyright © ElevenPlusExams.co.uk 2018

Second edition

All rights reserved. No part of this publication may be reproduced, stored or introduced into a retrieval system or transmitted in any form or by any means, without the prior written permission of the publisher nor may be circulated in any form of binding or cover other than the one in which it was published and without a similar condition including this condition being imposed on the subsequent publisher.

About Us

At Eleven Plus Exams, we supply high-quality 11 plus tuition for your children. Our website at **www.elevenplusexams.co.uk** is the largest website in the UK that specifically prepares children for the 11 plus exams. We also provide online services to schools and our **First Past The Post®** range of books has been well-received by schools, tuition centres and parents.

Eleven Plus Exams is recognised as a trusted and authoritative source. We have been quoted in numerous national newspapers, including *The Telegraph*, *The Observer*, the *Daily Mail* and *The Sunday Telegraph*, as well as on national television (BBC1 and Channel 4), and BBC radio.

Our website offers a vast amount of information and advice on the 11 plus, including a moderated online forum, books, downloadable material and online services to enhance your child's chances of success. Set up in 2004, the website grew from an initial 20 webpages to more than 65,000 today, and has been visited by millions of parents. It is moderated by experts in the field, who provide support for parents both before and after the exams.

Don't forget to visit **www.elevenplusexams.co.uk** and see why we are the market's leading one-stop shop for all your 11 plus needs. You will find:

- ✓ Comprehensive quality content and advice written by 11 plus experts
- ✓ Eleven Plus Exams online shop supplying a wide range of practice books, e-papers, software and apps
- ✓ Lots of FREE practice papers to download
- ✓ Professional tuition service
- ✓ Short revision courses
- ✓ Year-long 11 plus courses
- ✓ Mock exams tailored to reflect those of the main examining bodies

Other Titles in the First Past The Post® Series
11+ Essentials Range of Books

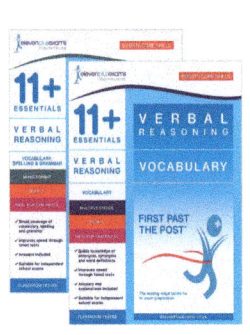

978-1-912364-60-2	Verbal Reasoning: Cloze Tests Book 1 - Mixed Format
978-1-912364-61-9	Verbal Reasoning: Cloze Tests Book 2 - Mixed Format
978-1-912364-78-7	Verbal Reasoning: Cloze Tests Book 3 - Mixed Format
978-1-912364-79-4	Verbal Reasoning: Cloze Tests Book 4 - Mixed Format
978-1-912364-62-6	Verbal Reasoning: Vocabulary Book 1 - Multiple Choice
978-1-912364-63-3	Verbal Reasoning: Vocabulary Book 2 - Multiple Choice
978-1-912364-64-0	Verbal Reasoning: Vocabulary Book 3 - Multiple Choice
978-1-912364-65-7	Verbal Reasoning: Vocabulary, Spelling and Grammar Book 1 - Multiple Choice
978-1-912364-66-4	Verbal Reasoning: Vocabulary, Spelling and Grammar Book 2 - Multiple Choice
978-1-912364-68-8	Verbal Reasoning: Vocabulary in Context Level 1
978-1-912364-69-5	Verbal Reasoning: Vocabulary in Context Level 2
978-1-912364-70-1	Verbal Reasoning: Vocabulary in Context Level 3
978-1-912364-71-8	Verbal Reasoning: Vocabulary in Context Level 4
978-1-912364-74-9	Verbal Reasoning: Vocabulary Puzzles Book 1
978-1-912364-75-6	Verbal Reasoning: Vocabulary Puzzles Book 2
978-1-912364-76-3	Verbal Reasoning: Practice Papers Book 1 - Multiple Choice

978-1-912364-02-2	English: Comprehensions Classic Literature Book 1 - Multiple Choice
978-1-912364-05-3	English: Comprehensions Contemporary Literature Book 1 - Multiple Choice
978-1-912364-08-4	English: Comprehensions Non-Fiction Book 1 - Multiple Choice
978-1-912364-14-5	English: Mini Comprehensions - Inference Book 1
978-1-912364-15-2	English: Mini Comprehensions - Inference Book 2
978-1-912364-16-9	English: Mini Comprehensions - Inference Book 3
978-1-912364-11-4	English: Mini Comprehensions - Fact-Finding Book 1
978-1-912364-12-1	English: Mini Comprehensions - Fact-Finding Book 2
978-1-912364-21-3	English: Spelling, Punctuation and Grammar Book 1
978-1-912364-00-8	English: Practice Papers Book 1 - Multiple Choice
978-1-912364-17-6	Creative Writing Examples

978-1-912364-30-5	Numerical Reasoning: Quick-Fire Book 1
978-1-912364-31-2	Numerical Reasoning: Quick-Fire Book 2
978-1-912364-32-9	Numerical Reasoning: Quick-Fire Book 1 - Multiple Choice
978-1-912364-33-6	Numerical Reasoning: Quick-Fire Book 2 - Multiple Choice
978-1-912364-34-3	Numerical Reasoning: Multi-Part Book 1
978-1-912364-35-0	Numerical Reasoning: Multi-Part Book 2
978-1-912364-36-7	Numerical Reasoning: Multi-Part Book 1 - Multiple Choice
978-1-912364-37-4	Numerical Reasoning: Multi-Part Book 2 - Multiple Choice

978-1-912364-43-5	Mathematics: Mental Arithmetic Book 1
978-1-912364-44-2	Mathematics: Mental Arithmetic Book 2
978-1-912364-45-9	Mathematics: Worded Problems Book 1
978-1-912364-46-6	Mathematics: Worded Problems Book 2
978-1-912364-52-7	Mathematics: Worded Problems Book 3
978-1-912364-47-3	Mathematics: Dictionary Plus
978-1-912364-50-3	Mathematics: Crossword Puzzles Book 1
978-1-912364-51-0	Mathematics: Crossword Puzzles Book 2
978-1-912364-48-0	Mathematics: Practice Papers Book 1 - Multiple Choice

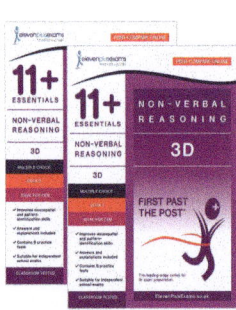

978-1-912364-87-9	Non-Verbal Reasoning: 2D Book 1 - Multiple Choice
978-1-912364-88-6	Non-Verbal Reasoning: 2D Book 2 - Multiple Choice
978-1-912364-85-5	Non-Verbal Reasoning: 3D Book 1 - Multiple Choice
978-1-912364-86-2	Non-Verbal Reasoning: 3D Book 2 - Multiple Choice
978-1-912364-83-1	Non-Verbal Reasoning: Practice Papers Book 1 - Multiple Choice

Contents

Sequences	1
Analogies	5
Codes	9
Similarities	13
Odd One Out	17
Complete the Square Grid	21
Complete the Grid	25
Reflections	29
Rotations	33
Hidden Shapes	37
Identify the Pair	41
Combine the Shapes	45
Rotation Analogies	49
Reflection Analogies	53
Cross Sections	57
Answers & Explanations	61

This workbook comprises 15 sections, each testing a different question style.

Each section comprises 10 questions.

BLANK PAGE

FIRST PAST THE POST

Sequences

In this section, you are asked to determine which of the options on the right best fits in place of the missing pattern in the series on the left. Each sequence follows a rule or set of rules regarding elements of the shapes within the series, for example: style, size, position, shading, orientation, angle, a repeating or alternating pattern, etc. Finding the correct answer involves working out the rules behind the sequence and applying it to find the missing pattern.

Example:

Which of the options best fits in place of the missing pattern in the series?

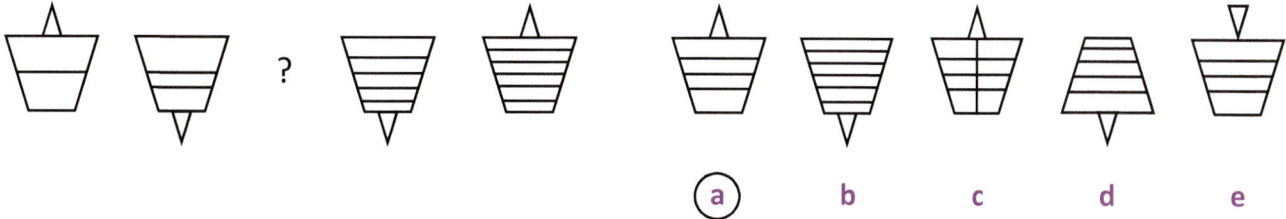

Answer: a

Explanation:

At each step, the isosceles triangle alternates from appearing on the top to the bottom of the trapezium, with its base always touching the trapezium. The number of horizontal lines within the trapezium increases by one at each step.

The missing figure must have an isosceles triangle with the base touching the top of the trapezium. It must also have three horizontal lines within the trapezium.

Therefore, the answer is a.

Sequences

Which of the options best fits in place of the missing pattern in the series?

1

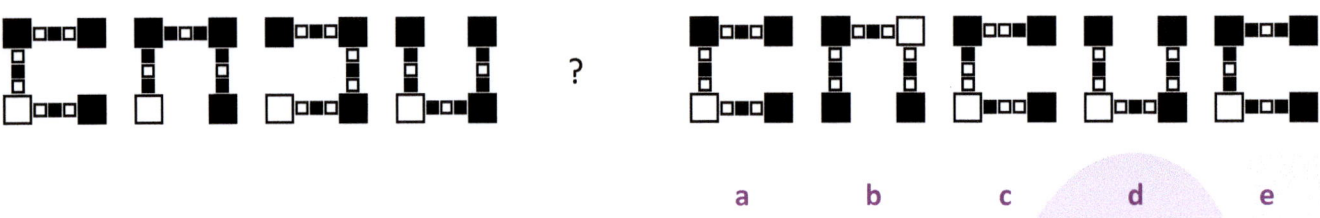

                                                              a   b   c   d   e

2

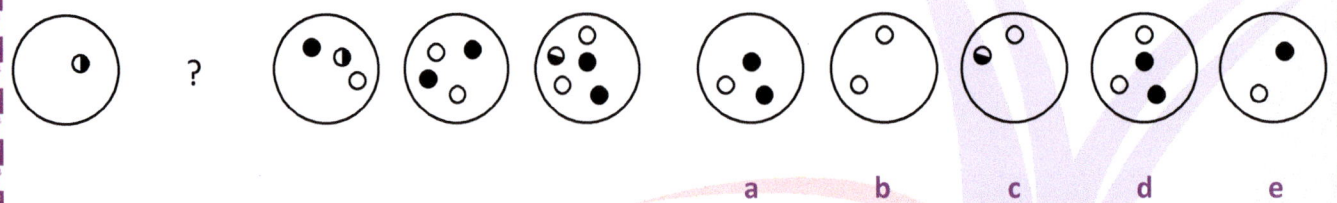

                                                              a   b   c   d   e

3

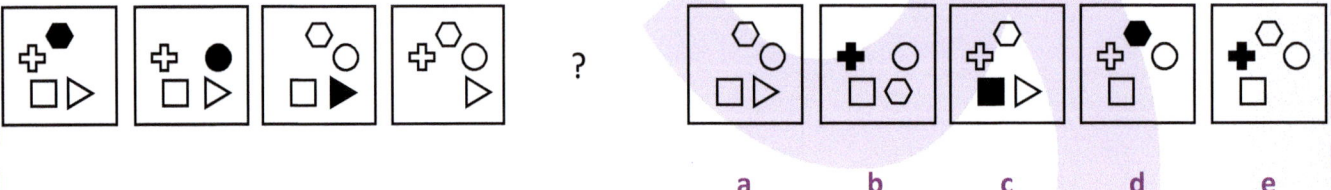

                                                              a   b   c   d   e

4

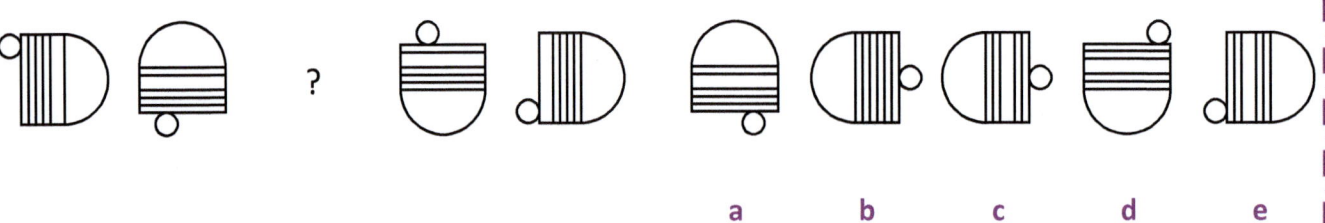

                                                              a   b   c   d   e

Sequences

Which of the options best fits in place of the missing pattern in the series?

5

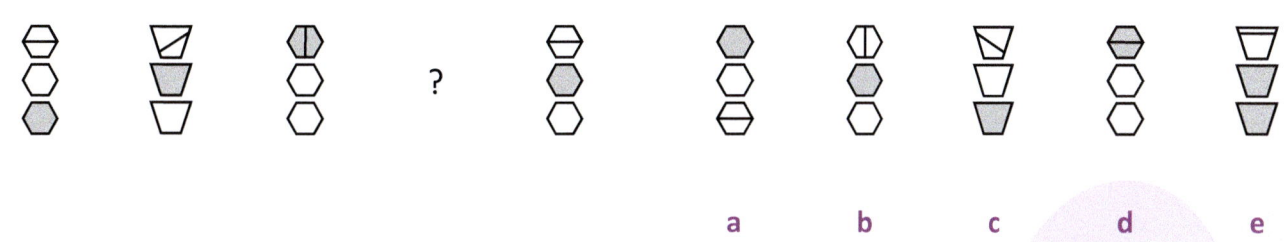

         a   b   c   d   e

6

7

8

Sequences

Which of the options best fits in place of the missing pattern in the series?

9

a b c d e

10

a b c d e

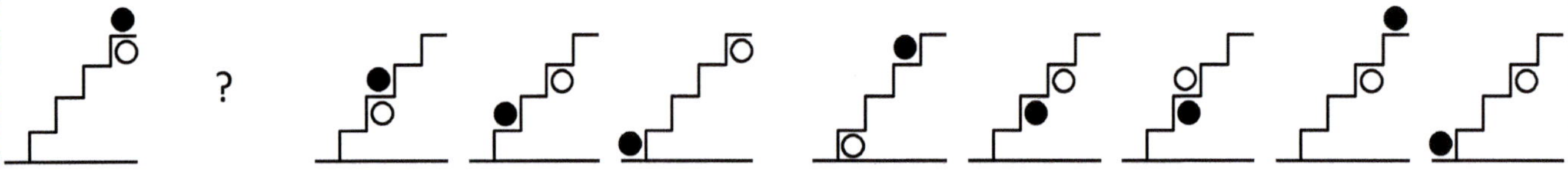

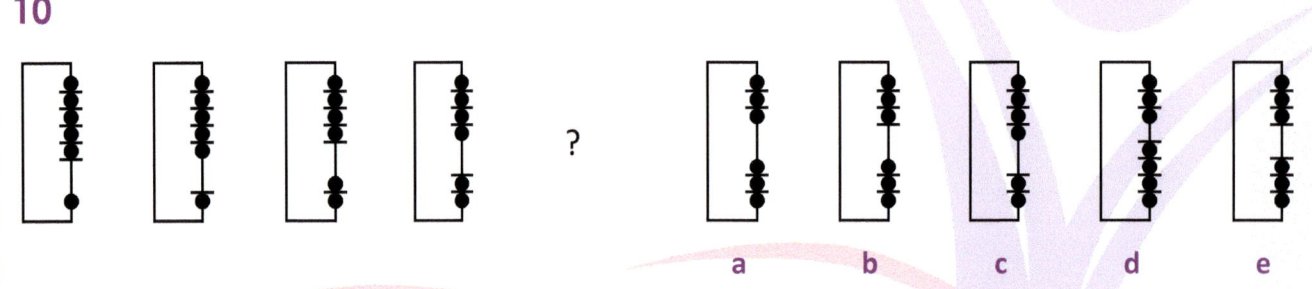

Analogies

In this section, you are asked to determine which shape completes the pair on the right in the same way as the pair(s) on the left. The second pair must be completed using the same rule(s) as in the first pair.

The second shape in a pair can differ from the first shape in terms of size, position, shading, orientation, angle, etc.

Example:

Which shape or pattern completes the pair on the right in the same way as the pair(s) on the left?

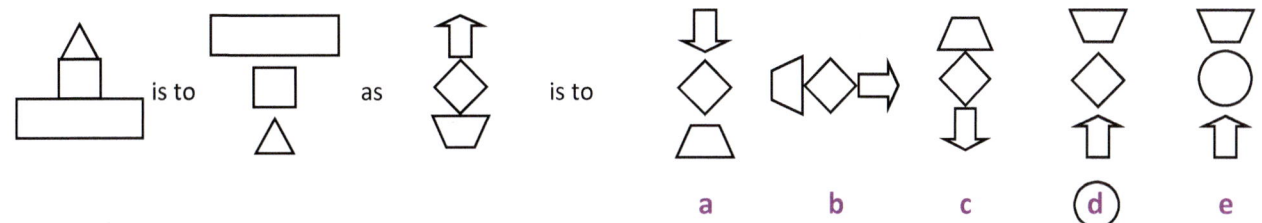

Answer: d

Explanation:

The top and bottom shapes swap positions but remain in the same orientation, and gaps are introduced so that none of the shapes touch.

The trapezium and arrow swap positions but remain in the same orientation and gaps are introduced.

Therefore, the answer is d.

Analogies

Which shape or pattern completes the pair on the right in the same way as the pair(s) on the left?

1

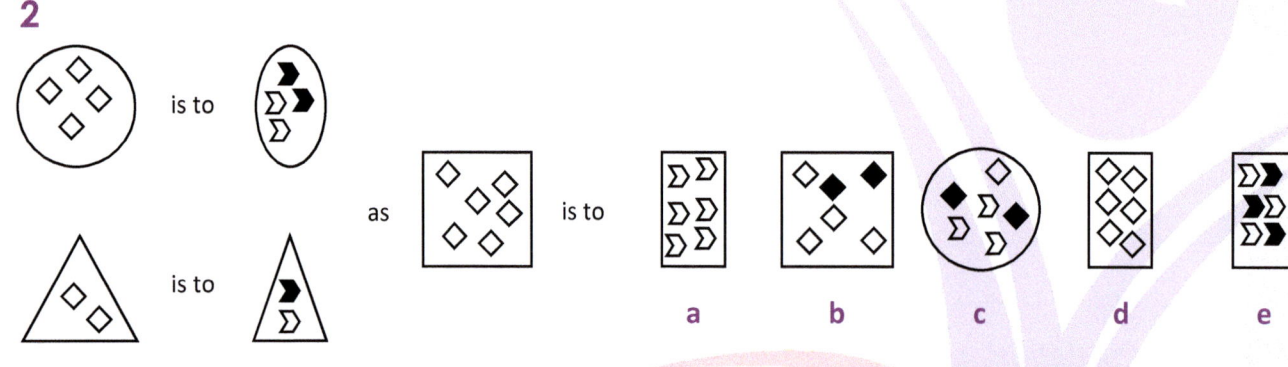

2

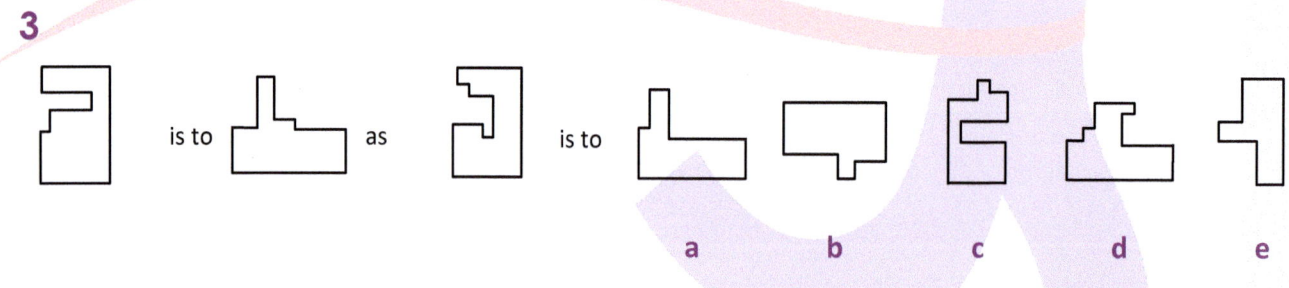

3

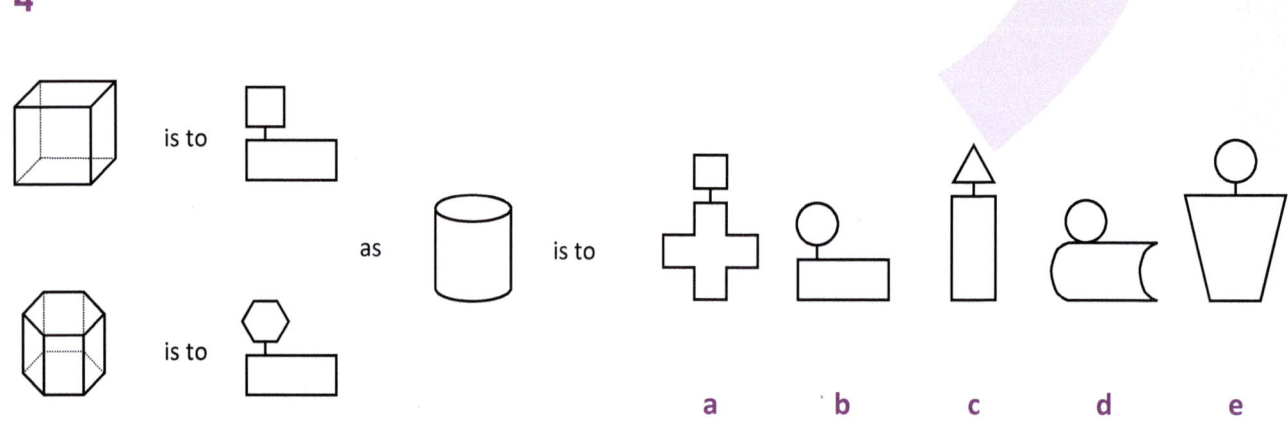

4

Analogies

Which shape or pattern completes the pair on the right in the same way as the pair(s) on the left?

5

6

7

8

Analogies

Which shape or pattern completes the pair on the right in the same way as the pair(s) on the left?

9
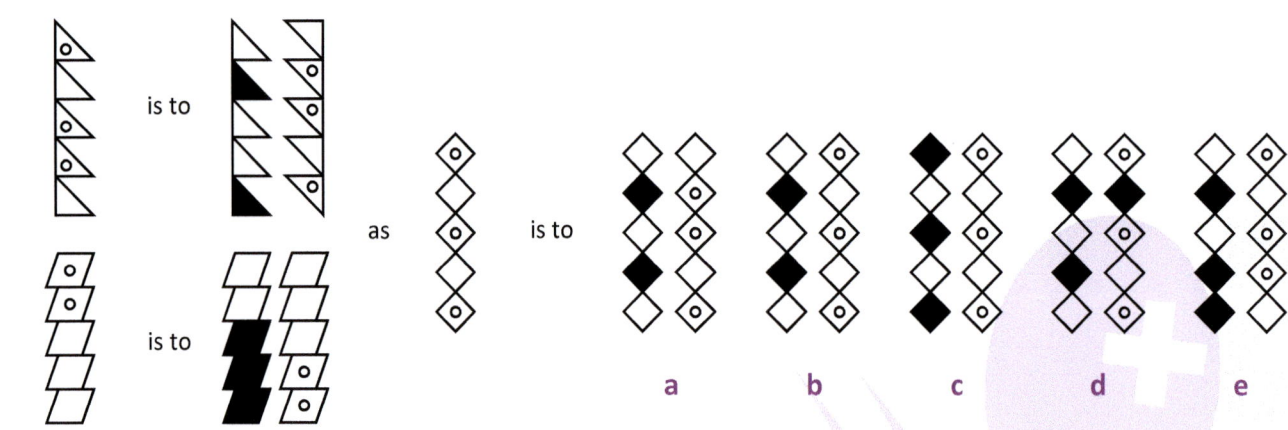

a   b   c   d   e

10
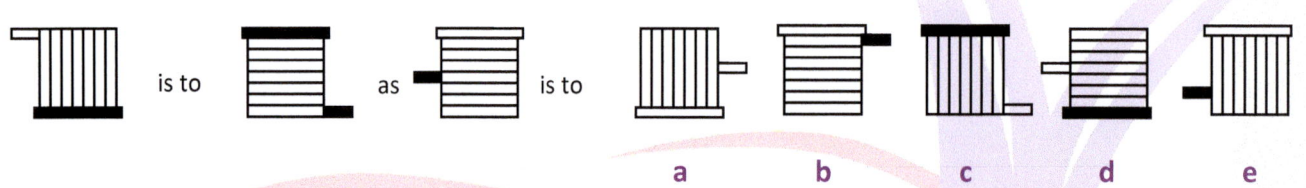

a   b   c   d   e

FIRST PAST THE POST

Codes

In this section, you are asked to determine which of the codes on the right corresponds to the final pattern on the left. Each letter of the code represents a particular element of the shapes in the series, for example: style, size, position, shading, orientation, angle, etc. Finding the correct answer involves working out the rule(s) behind the codes using the patterns already given.

Example:

Which code corresponds to the final pattern?

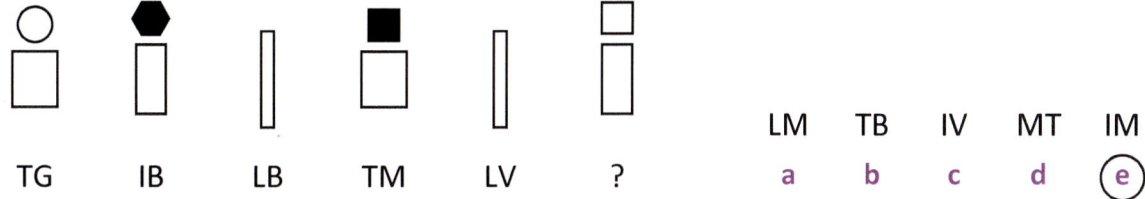

Answer: e

Explanation:

First letter = rectangle style: L (tallest), I (second tallest), T (shortest)

Second letter = shape on top of rectangle: B (hexagon), G (circle), M (square), V (pentagon)

The shape consists of the second tallest rectangle and a square on top of it, so the code is IM.

Therefore, the answer is e.

Codes

Which code corresponds to the final pattern?

1

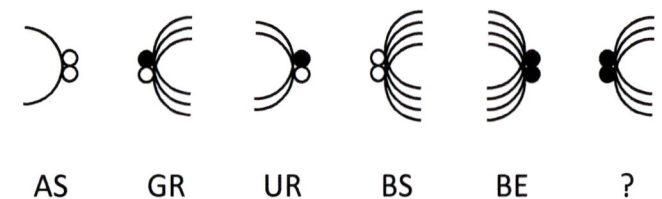

AS GR UR BS BE ?

GS	BR	GE	UG	AE
a	b	c	d	e

2

TR BD PR TX BS ?

PD	TB	PS	BX	TD
a	b	c	d	e

3

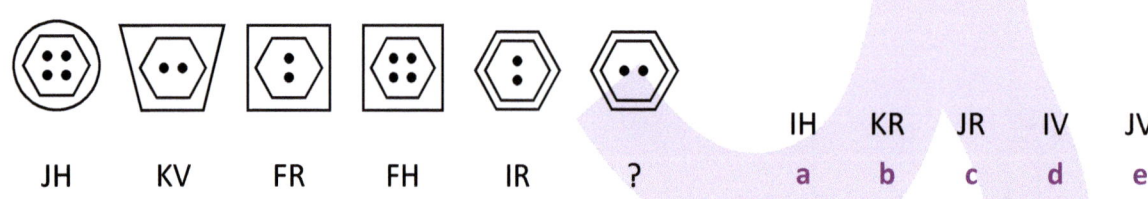

JH KV FR FH IR ?

IH	KR	JR	IV	JV
a	b	c	d	e

4

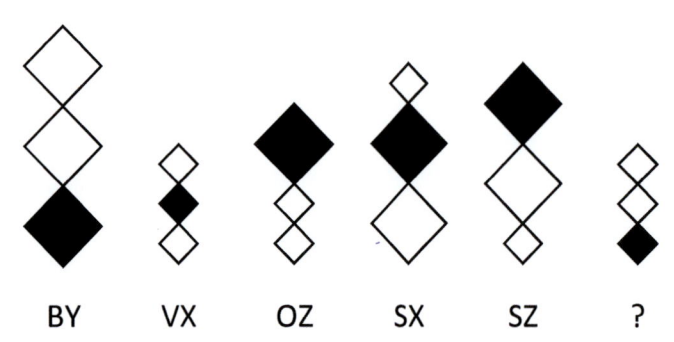

BY VX OZ SX SZ ?

OY	VZ	BX	VS	VY
a	b	c	d	e

Codes

Which code corresponds to the final pattern?

5

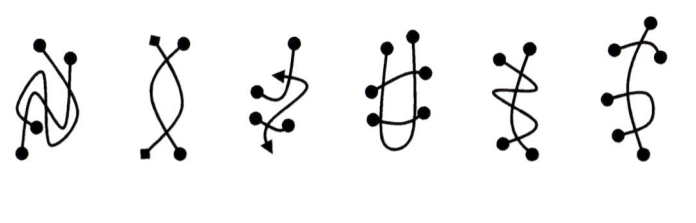

VC	VB	LB	LZ	VZ	?		VL	LC	LV	LD	ZC
							a	b	c	d	e

6

AF	WQ	MB	ML	WL	?		WA	WF	AB	MQ	AL
							a	b	c	d	e

7

 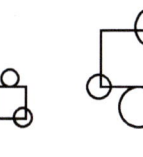  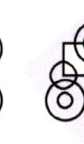

WX	MC	WE	OF	OX	?		WF	OE	ME	MF	OC
							a	b	c	d	e

8

QN	AO	EO	PN	QK	?		EN	PK	AN	QO	AK
							a	b	c	d	e

Codes

Which code corresponds to the final pattern?

9

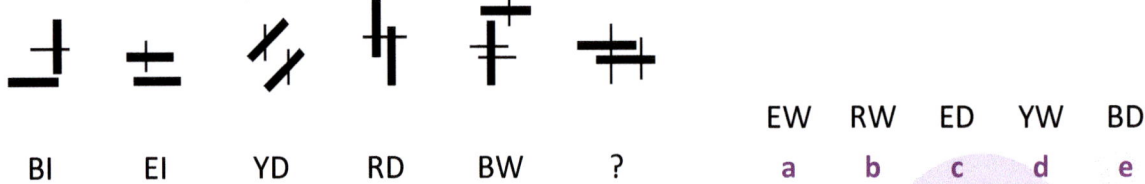

BI   EI   YD   RD   BW   ?

EW   RW   ED   YW   BD
a   b   c   d   e

10

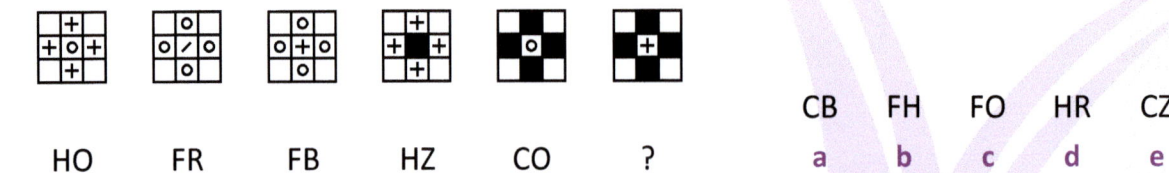

HO   FR   FB   HZ   CO   ?

CB   FH   FO   HR   CZ
a   b   c   d   e

FIRST PAST THE POST

Similarities

In this section, you are asked to determine which of the shapes on the right best belongs with the shapes on the left. The shape on the right that has the most in common with the shapes on the left will share elements such as style, size, position, shading, layering, orientation, angle, etc.

Example:

Which shape on the right goes best with the shapes on the left?

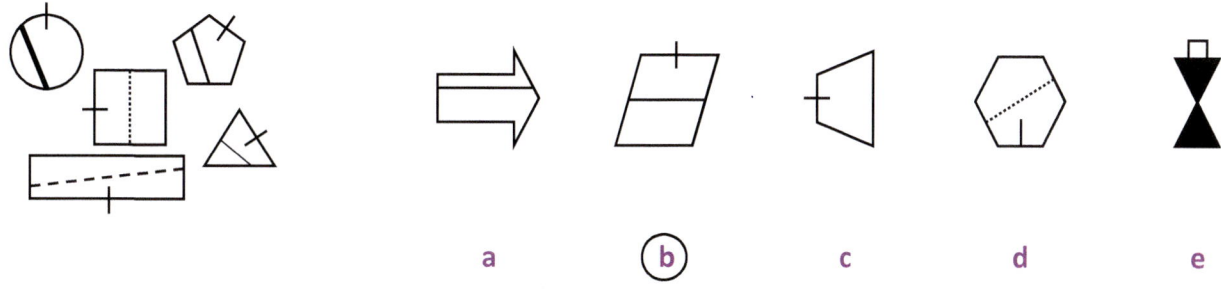

a   b   c   d   e

Answer: b

Explanation:

All the figures on the left have an internal straight line that touches the perimeter of the shape at each end. Each figure also has a shorter line which intersects a side of the shape.

Only option b has an internal line that touches the perimeter of the shape at both ends and a shorter line which intersects a side of the shape.

Similarities

Which shape on the right goes best with the shapes on the left?

1

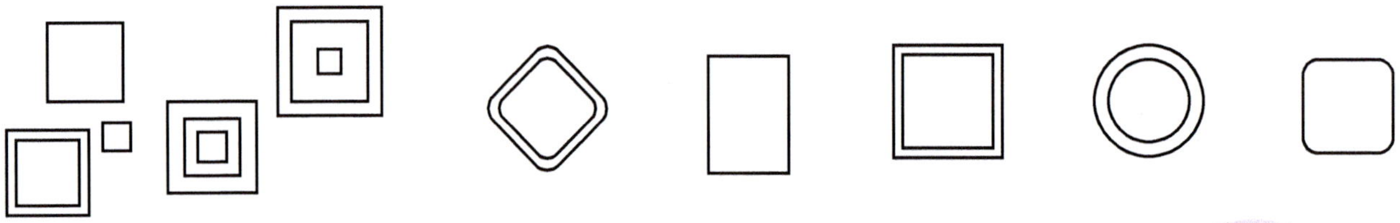

    a   b   c   d   e

2

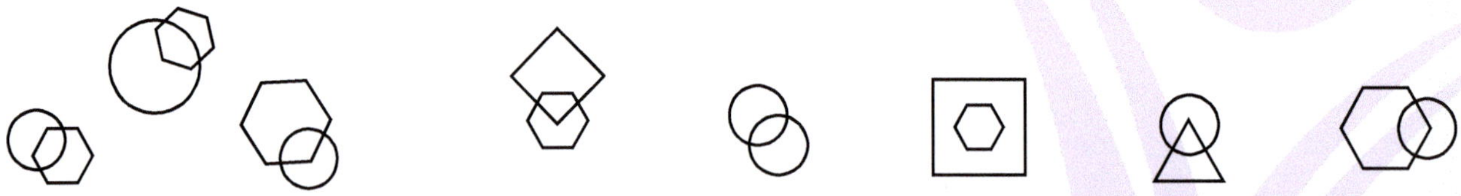

    a   b   c   d   e

3

    a   b   c   d   e

4

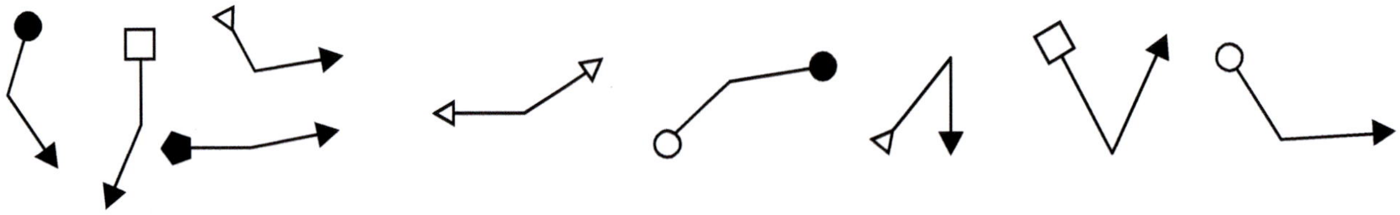

    a   b   c   d   e

Similarities

Which shape on the right goes best with the shapes on the left?

5

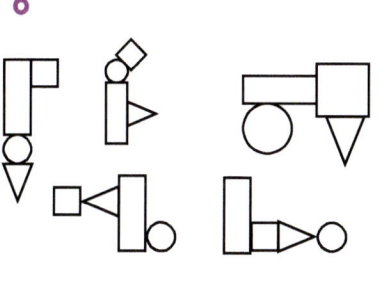   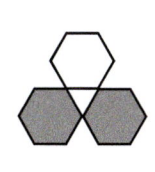   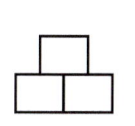   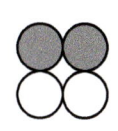   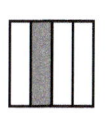   

                                        a   b   c   d   e

6

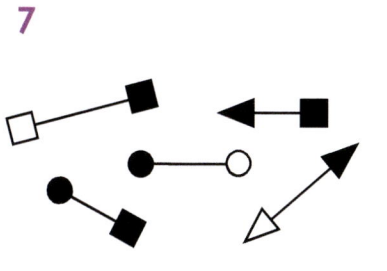   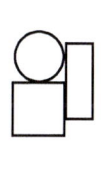      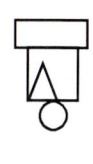   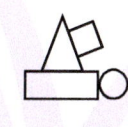   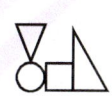

                                          a   b   c   d   e

7

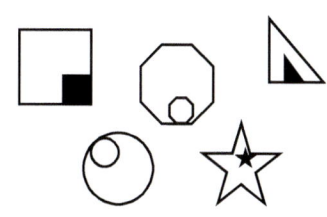   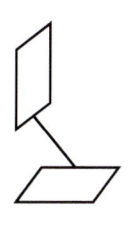   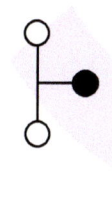   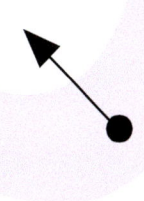   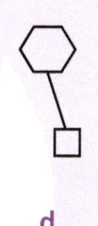   

                                        a   b   c   d   e

8

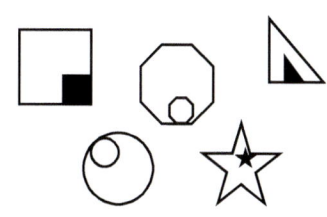   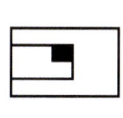      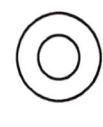   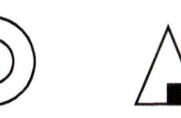   

                                        a   b   c   d   e

Similarities

Which shape on the right goes best with the shapes on the left?

9

  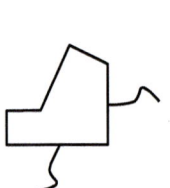  

      a   b   c   d   e

10

      a   b   c   d   e

FIRST PAST THE POST

Odd One Out

In this section, you are asked to find which of the five figures on each row is most unlike the others, or the odd one out.

This type of question tests your ability to determine the differences and similarities between shapes.

Reasons why a figure is the odd one out include its angle of rotation, shading style, reflection, size, position, or the number of shapes within it.

Example:

Which figure is the odd one out?

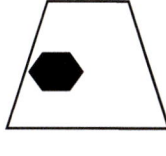 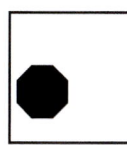 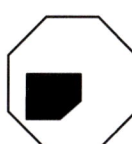 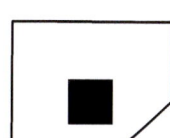 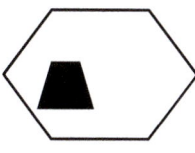

    a   b   c   d   e

Answer: d

Explanation:

In each figure, a shaded shape has been placed inside a different, larger shape.

In all figures but **d**, the shaded shape has been positioned on the left side of the larger shape.

Odd One Out

Which figure is the odd one out?

1

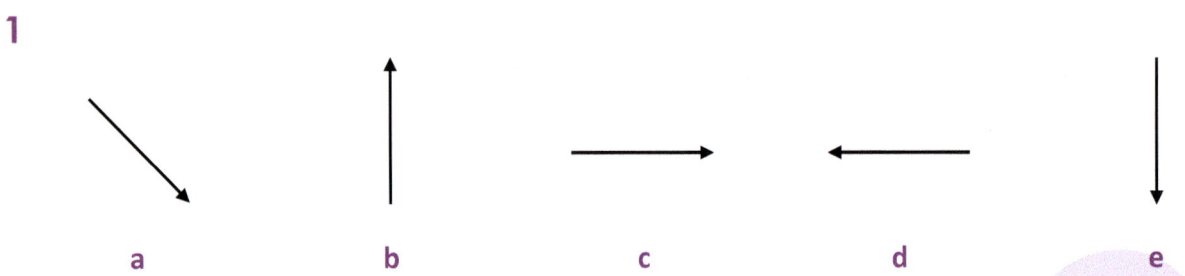

a   b   c   d   e

2

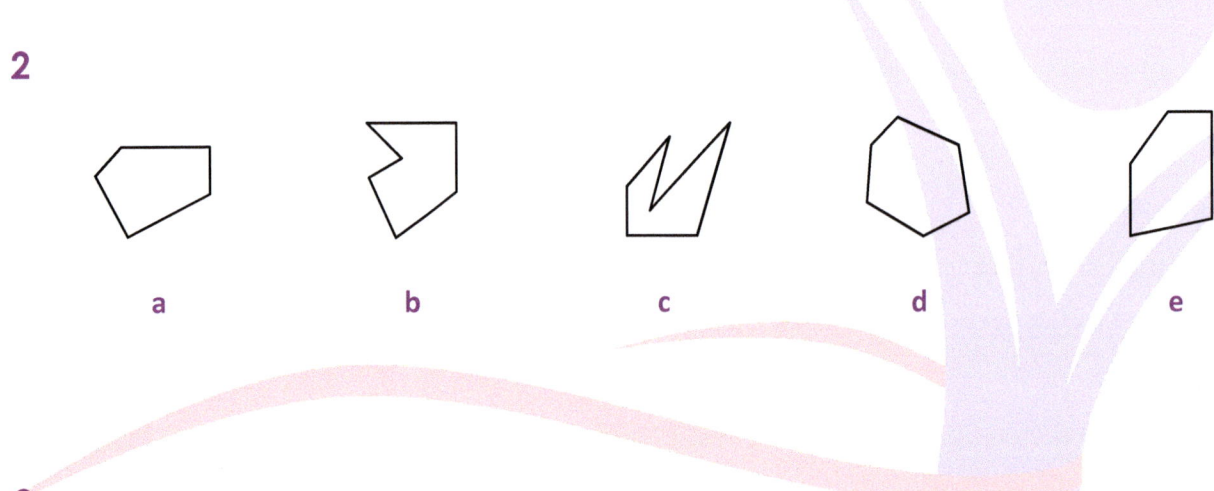

a   b   c   d   e

3

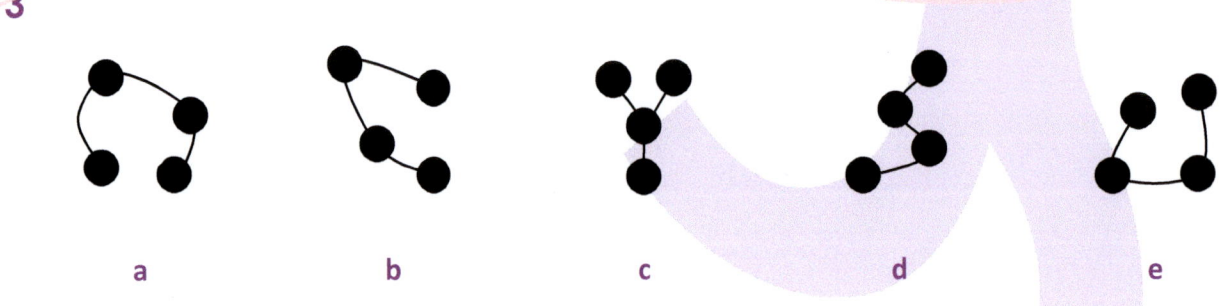

a   b   c   d   e

4

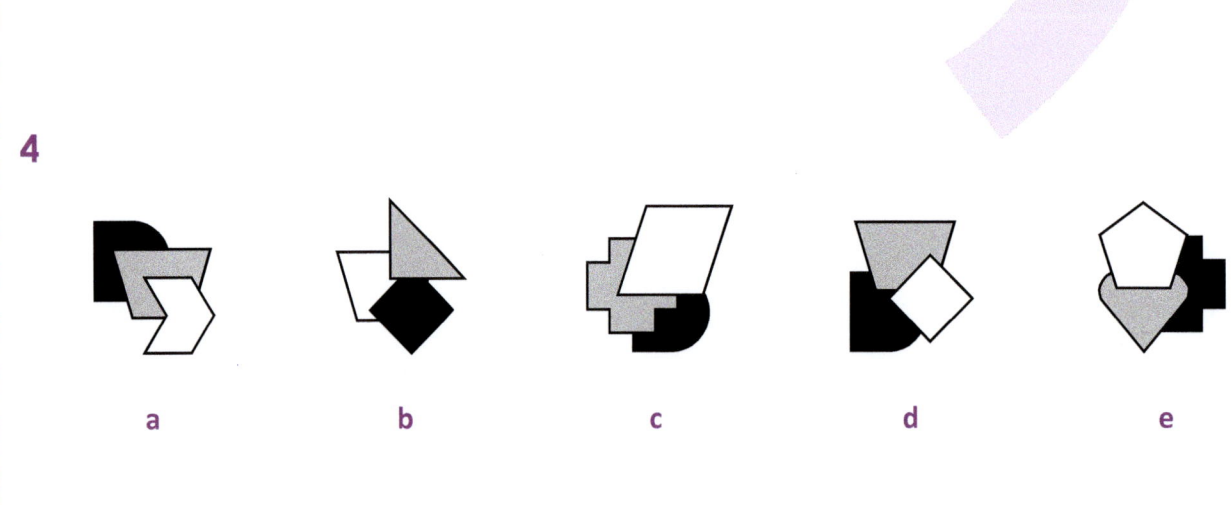

a   b   c   d   e

Odd One Out

Which figure is the odd one out?

5

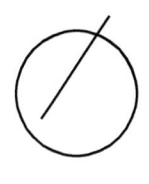 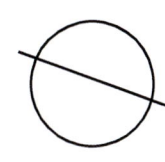 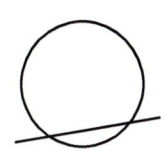 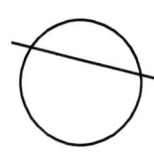 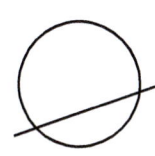

a　　　　　b　　　　　c　　　　　d　　　　　e

6

 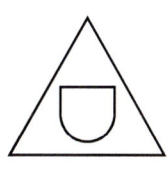 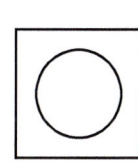 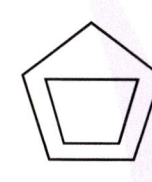 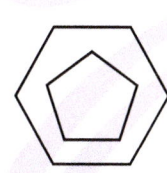

a　　　　　b　　　　　c　　　　　d　　　　　e

7

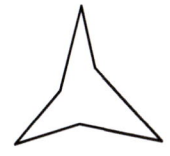 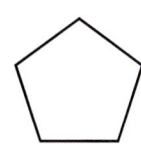 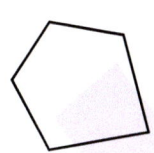 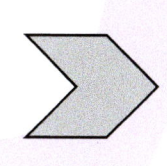 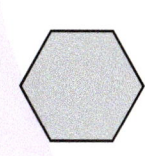

a　　　　　b　　　　　c　　　　　d　　　　　e

8

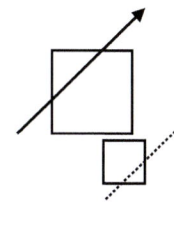 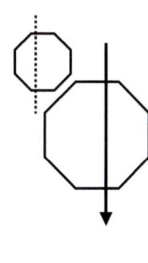 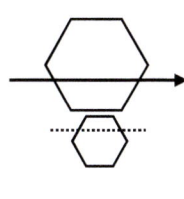 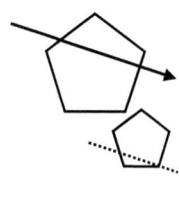 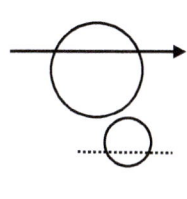

a　　　　　b　　　　　c　　　　　d　　　　　e

Odd One Out

Which figure is the odd one out?

9

   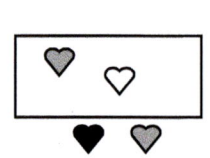 

a   b   c   d   e

10

   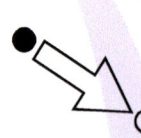 

a   b   c   d   e

FIRST PAST THE POST

Complete the Square Grid

In this section, you are asked to determine which of the options on the right best fits in place of the missing square in the grid on the left. Patterns in the grid may occur over rows or columns and will involve similarities in shape elements including style, size, position, shading, orientation, angle, etc. Sometimes the missing square will complete a reflective image in the grid or be a rotation of another square. Finding the correct answer involves working out which square best follows these rules and fits in the grid.

Example:

Which of the options best fits in place of the missing square in the grid?

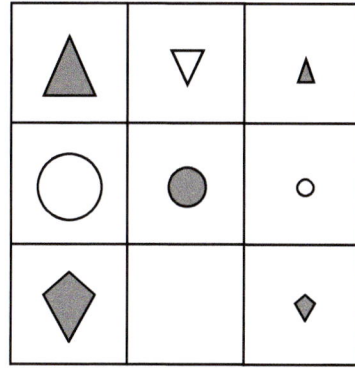      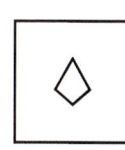   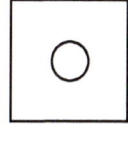   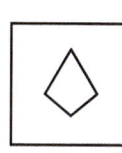

  a   b   c   d   e

Answer: c

Explanation:

Looking across each row, the shape decreases in size and alternates between shaded and unshaded. Alternate shapes in each row are inverted. The missing shape must be an unshaded, upside-down kite of intermediate size.

Therefore, the answer is **c**.

Complete the Square Grid

Which of the options best fits in place of the missing square in the grid?

1

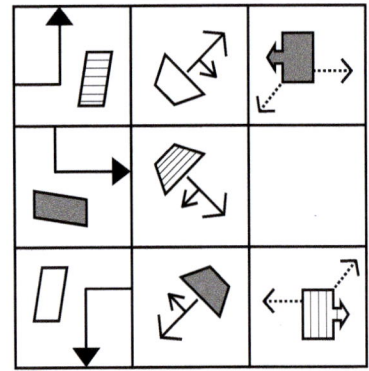   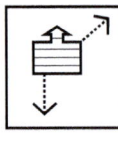   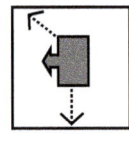   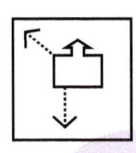   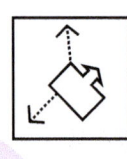

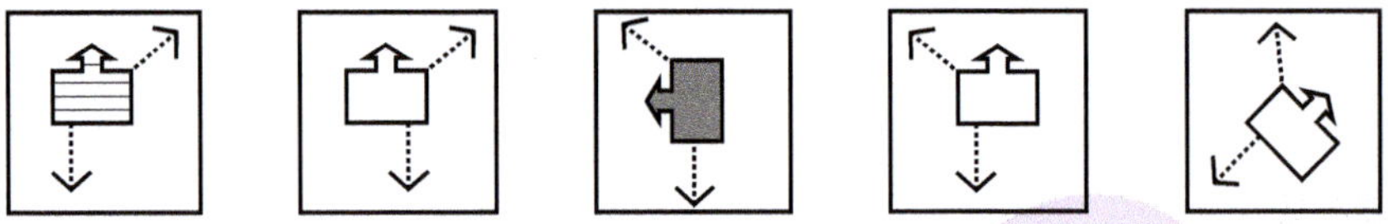

a　　　b　　　c　　　d　　　e

2

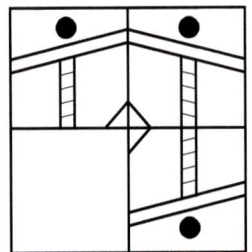   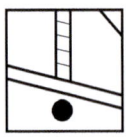   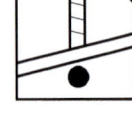   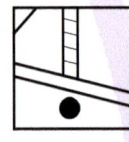   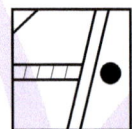

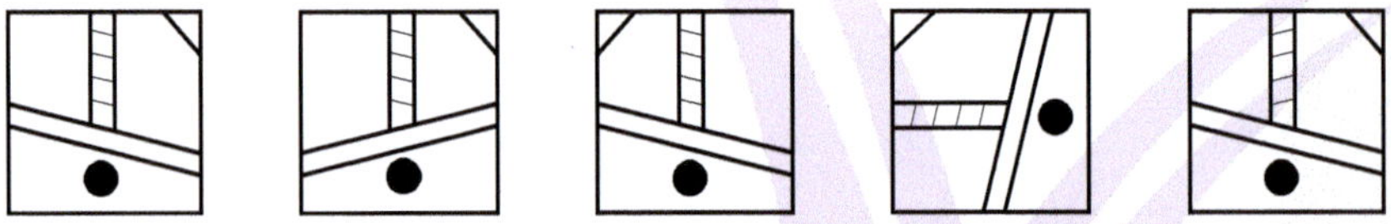

a　　　b　　　c　　　d　　　e

3

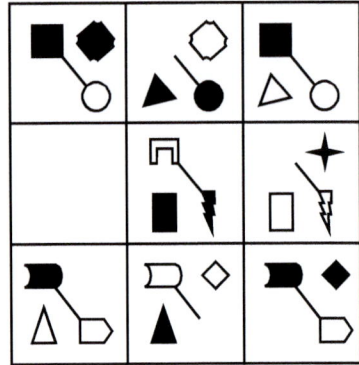         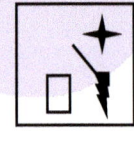      

a　　　b　　　c　　　d　　　e

4

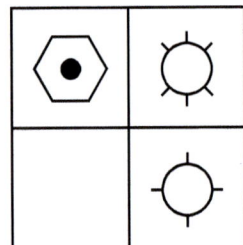      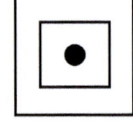   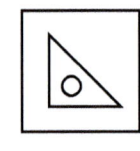   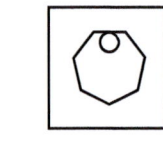   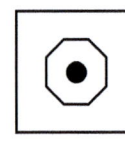

a　　　b　　　c　　　d　　　e

Complete the Square Grid

Which of the options best fits in place of the missing square in the grid?

5

 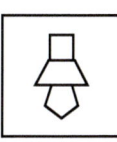 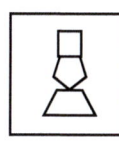 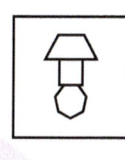

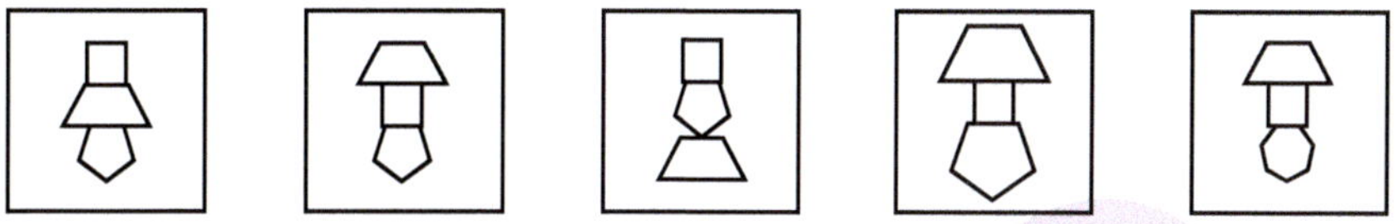

a   b   c   d   e

6

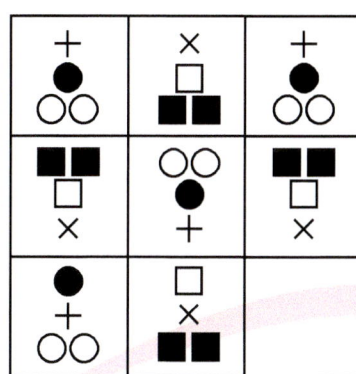 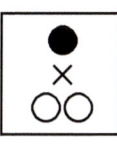 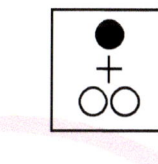 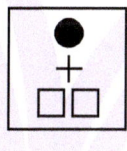

a   b   c   d   e

7

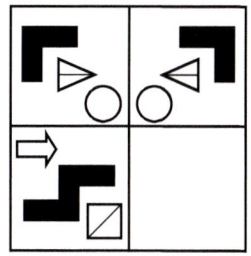 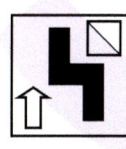   

a   b   c   d   e

8

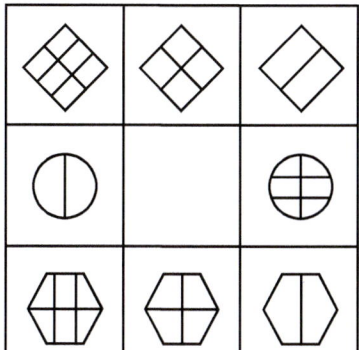 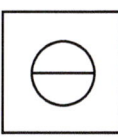 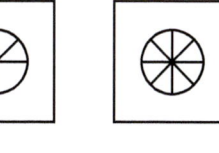 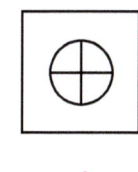 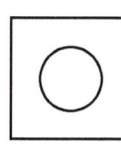

a   b   c   d   e

© 2018 ElevenPlusExams.co.uk   COPYING STRICTLY PROHIBITED

Complete the Square Grid

Which of the options best fits in place of the missing square in the grid?

9

         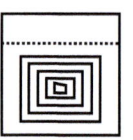   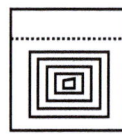

a   b   c   d   e

10
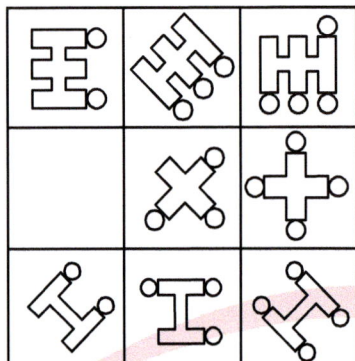

   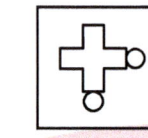   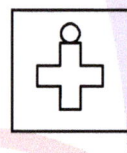   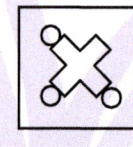   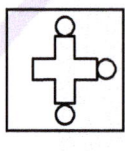

a   b   c   d   e

FIRST PAST THE POST

Complete the Grid

In this section, you are asked to determine which of the options on the right best fits in place of the missing section in the grid on the left. Patterns in the grid may occur in a clockwise or anticlockwise cycle around the grid and will involve similarities in shape elements including style, size, position, shading, orientation, angle, etc. Sometimes the missing section will complete a reflective image in the grid or be a rotation of another section. Finding the correct answer involves working out which option best follows these rules and fits in the grid.

Example:

Which of the options best fits in place of the missing section in the grid?

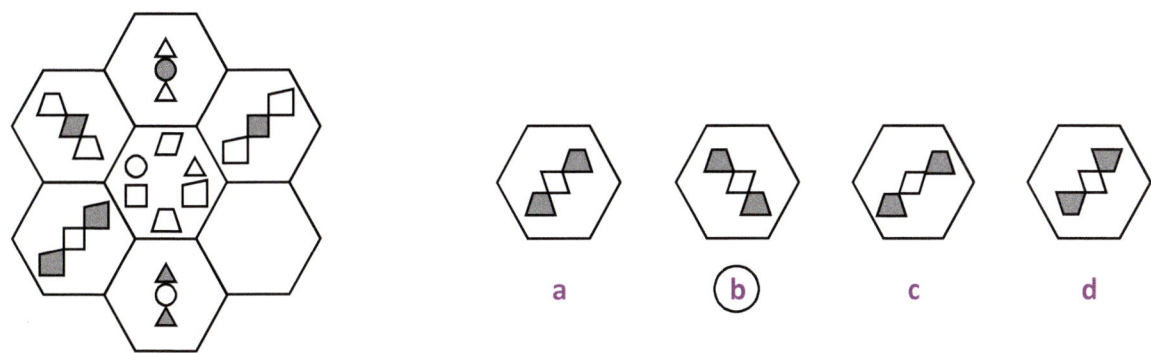

Answer: b

Explanation:

The hexagons directly opposite each other in the grid contain identical shapes apart from their shading style, which changes from shaded to unshaded and from unshaded to shaded.

Therefore, the answer is **b**.

Complete the Grid

Which of the options best fits in place of the missing section in the grid?

1

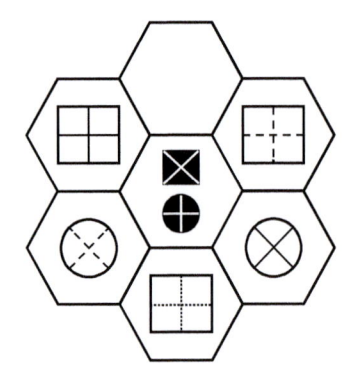

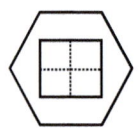  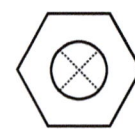 

a b c d

2

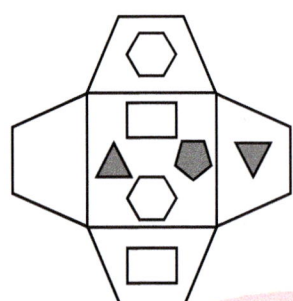

  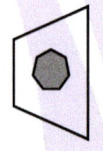

a b c d

3

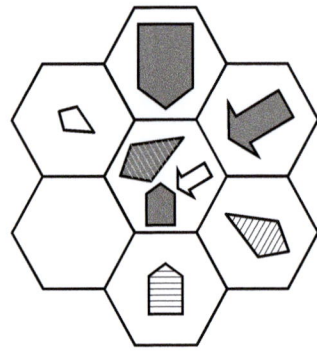

 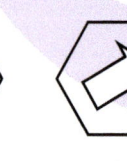 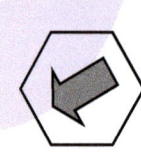 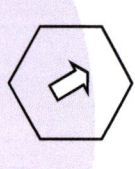

a b c d

4

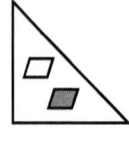  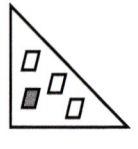 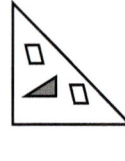

a b c d

Complete the Grid

Which of the options best fits in place of the missing section in the grid?

5

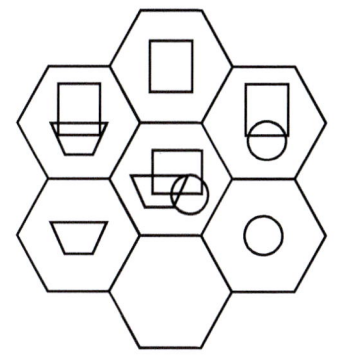

   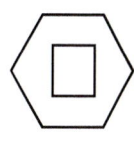      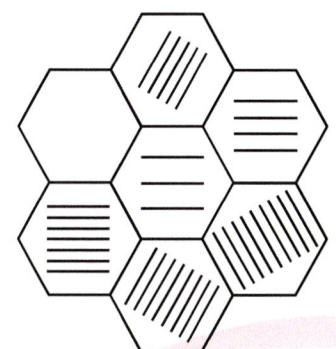

a   b   c   d

6

      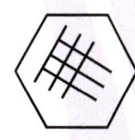   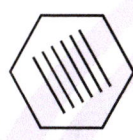

a   b   c   d

7

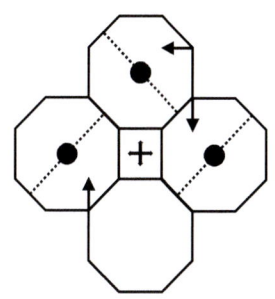

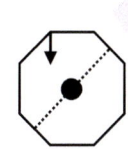   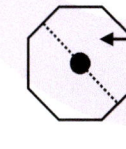   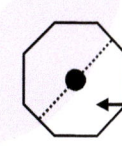   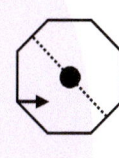

a   b   c   d

8

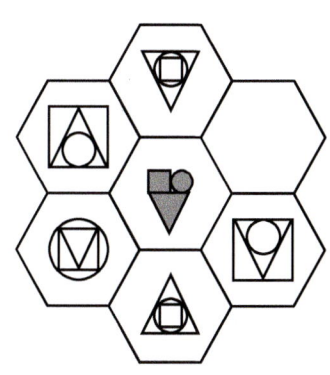

      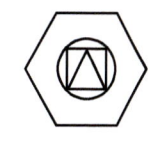   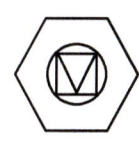

a   b   c   d

Complete the Grid

Which of the options best fits in place of the missing section in the grid?

9

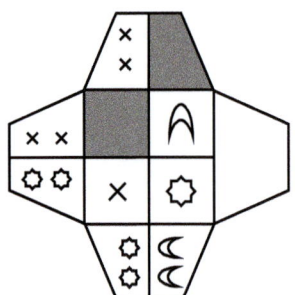

    a   b   c   d

10

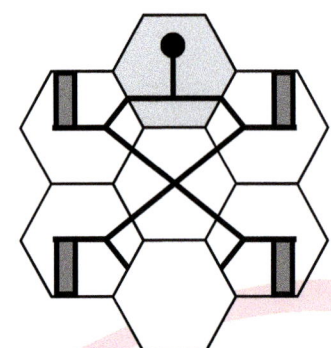

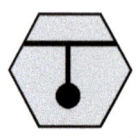 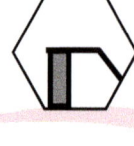  

    a   b   c   d

FIRST PAST THE POST

Reflections

In this section, you are asked to find which one of the four figures on the right is a mirror image, or a reflection of the figure on the left in a vertical mirror line.

Remember to concentrate on specific shape features such as a left-leaning line. The same line will appear right-leaning in the reflection. Also remember that most shapes when reflected do not give the same result as a rotation of the same shape.

Example:

Which figure on the right is the reflection of the figure on the left in a vertical mirror line?

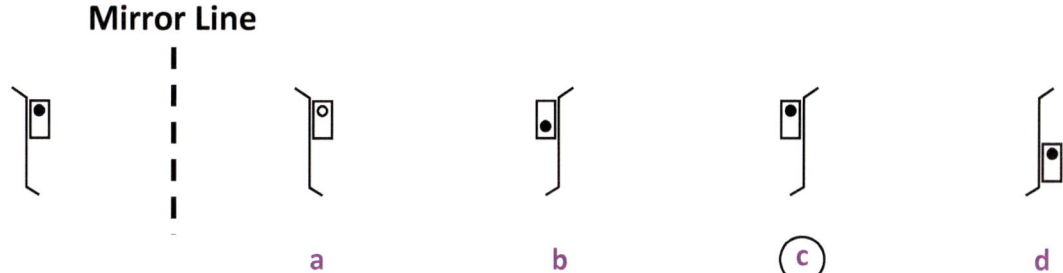

Answer: c

Explanation:

The left-leaning line will appear right-leaning in the reflection, as in answers b, c and d.

The rectangle and shaded circle will appear on the left of the vertical line in the reflection, as in answers b and c.

The shaded circle will be in the same position inside the rectangle in the reflection.

Therefore, the answer is **c**.

Reflections

Which figure on the right is the reflection of the figure on the left in a vertical mirror line?

1

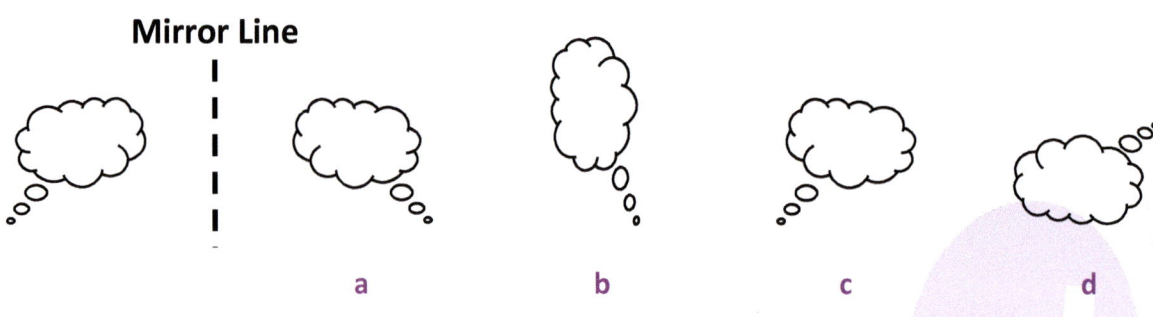

a b c d

2

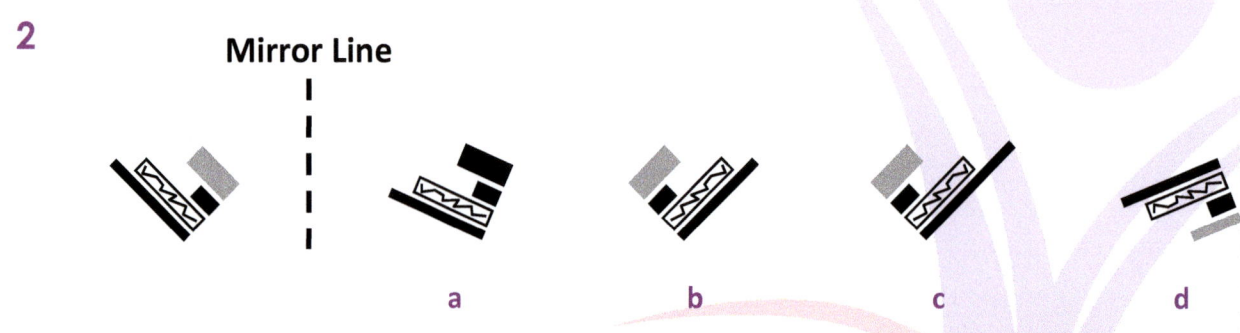

a b c d

3

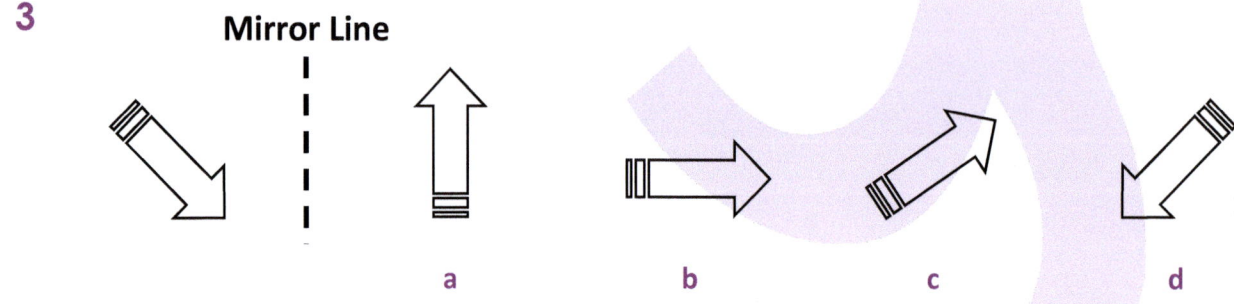

a b c d

4

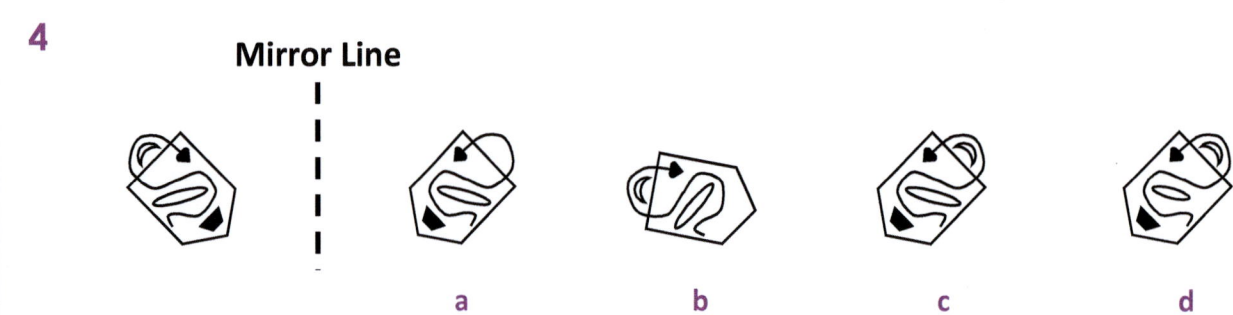

a b c d

Reflections

Which figure on the right is the reflection of the figure on the left in a vertical mirror line?

5 Mirror Line

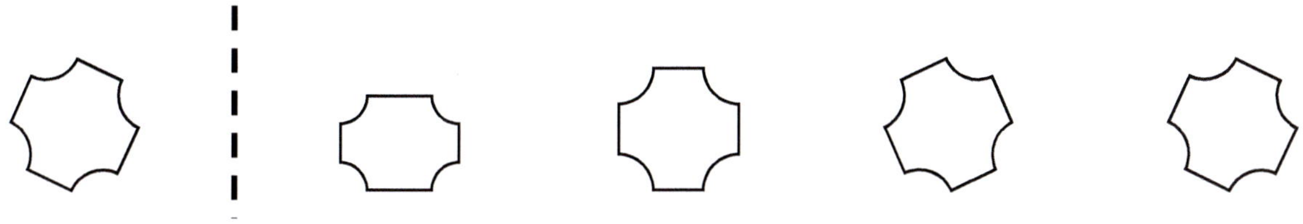

a   b   c   d

6 Mirror Line

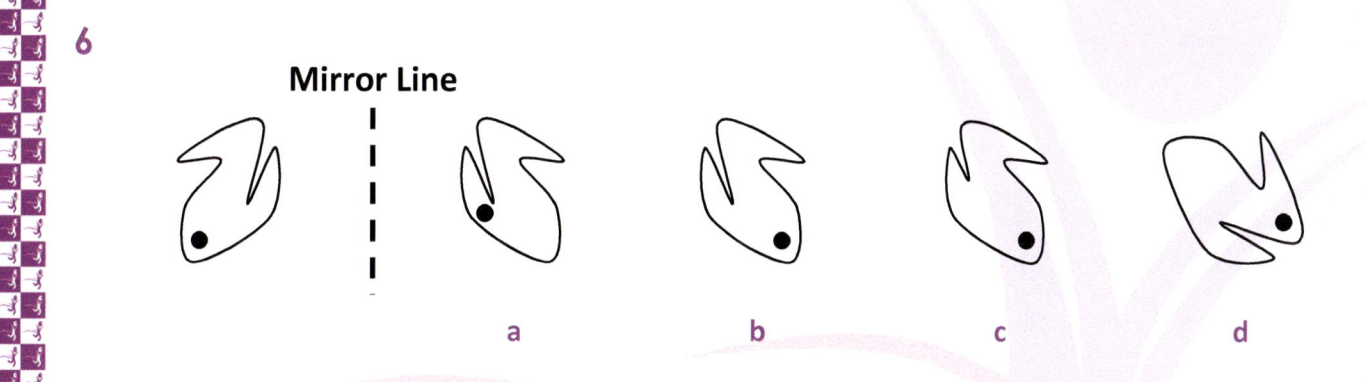

a   b   c   d

7 Mirror Line

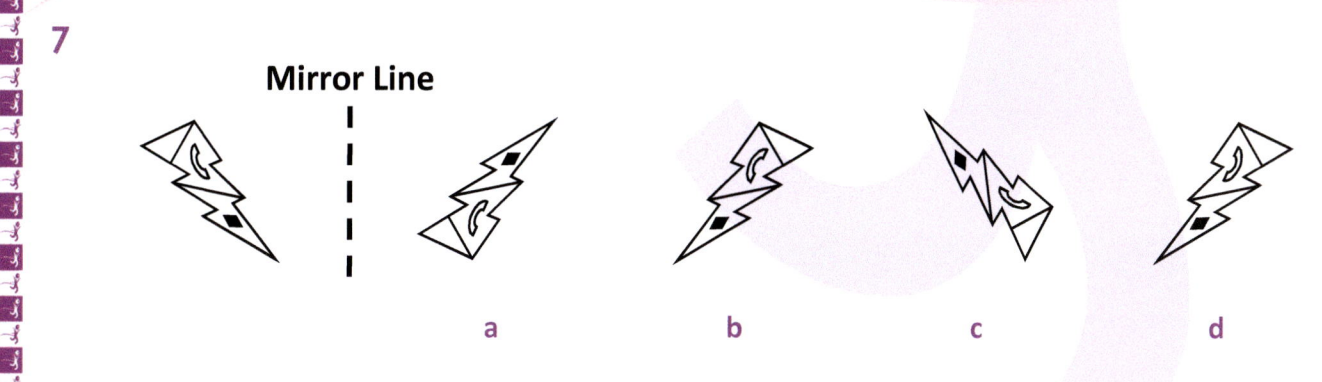

a   b   c   d

8 Mirror Line

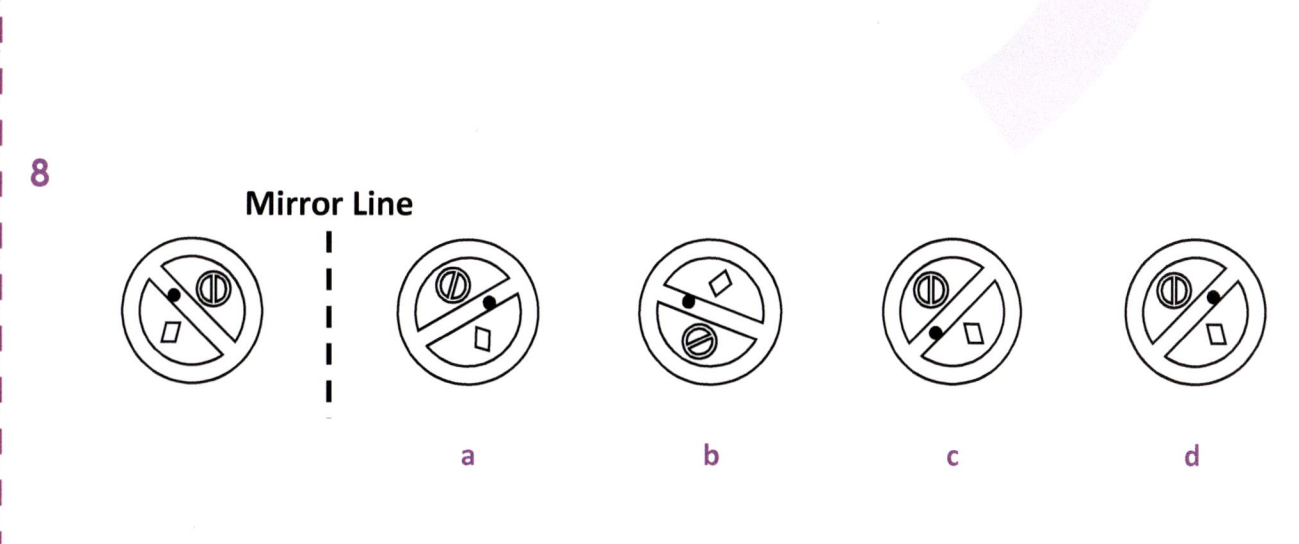

a   b   c   d

Reflections

Which figure on the right is the reflection of the figure on the left in a vertical mirror line?

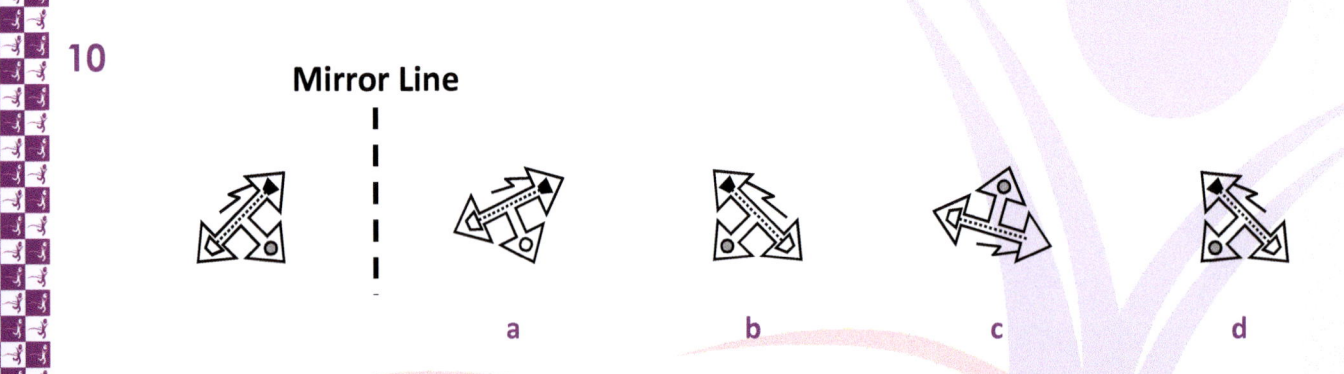

9

Mirror Line

a   b   c   d

10

Mirror Line

a   b   c   d

Rotations

In this section, you are asked to find which one of the four figures on the right is exactly the same as the figure on the left after a rotation has taken place.

Remember that most shapes, when rotated, do not give the same result as a reflection of the same shape.

Example:

Which figure on the right is a rotation of the figure on the left?

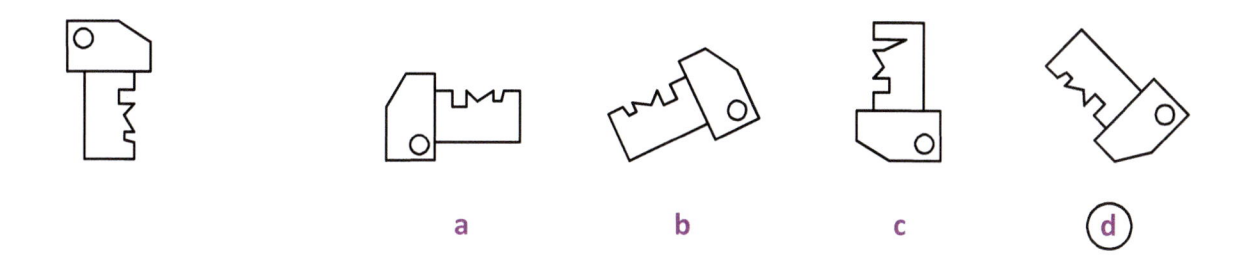

Answer: d

Explanation:

Option a has been rotated anticlockwise by 90 degrees but the circle is shown in the wrong corner.

The rotation in option b is of the figure's mirror image.

Option c has been rotated through 180 degrees but the jagged edge has a different pattern.

Option d shows a correct 135 degree clockwise rotation with no other changes to the original figure.

Rotations

Which figure on the right is a rotation of the figure on the left?

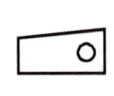

1

    a   b   c   d

2

    a   b   c   d

3

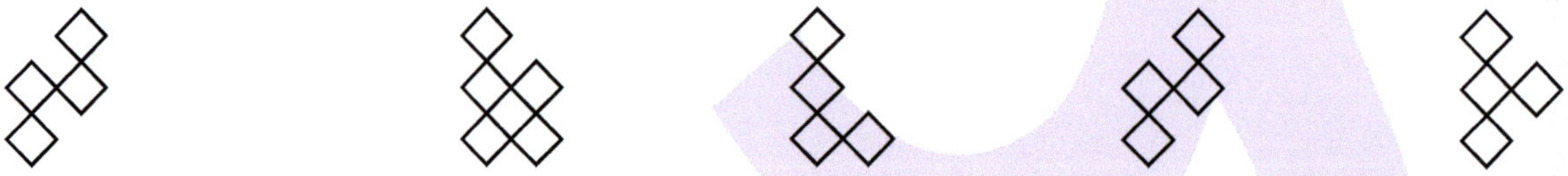

    a   b   c   d

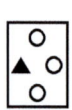

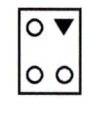

4

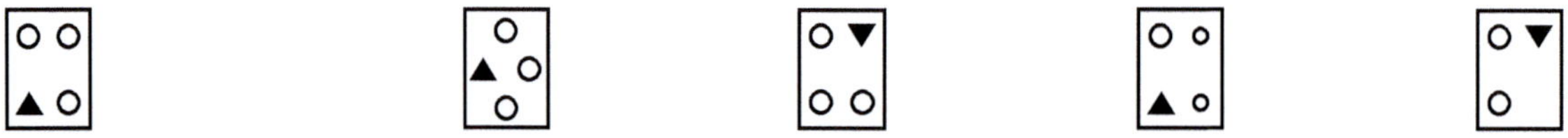

    a   b   c   d

Rotations

Which figure on the right is a rotation of the figure on the left?

5

   a   b   c   d

6

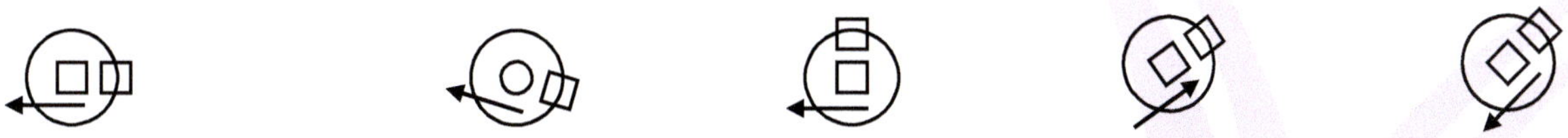

   a   b   c   d

7

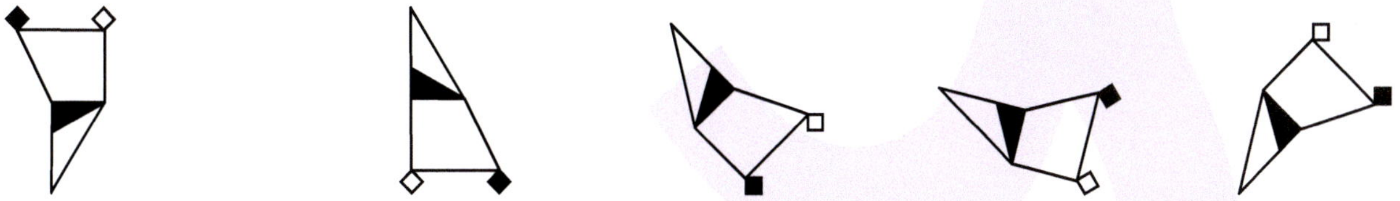

   a   b   c   d

8

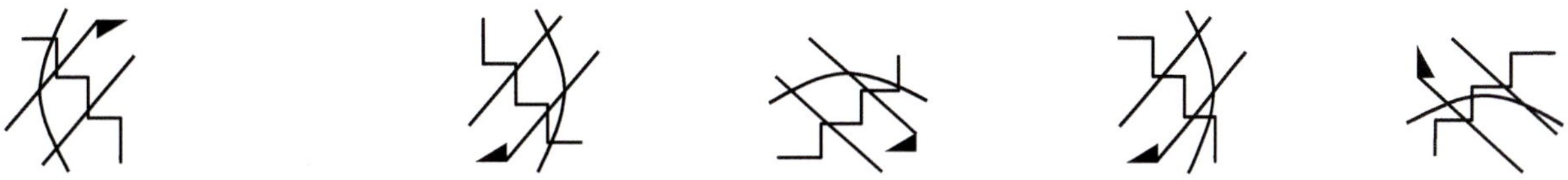

   a   b   c   d

Rotations

Which figure on the right is a rotation of the figure on the left?

9

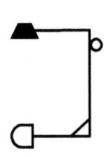

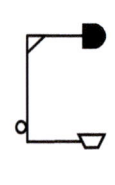

        a 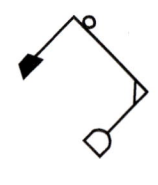   b 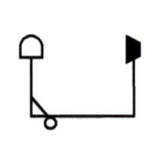   c 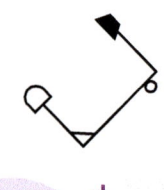   d

10

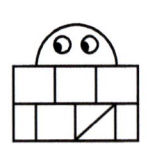

        a    b 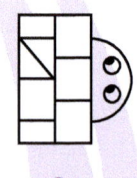   c    d

ND THE POST

Hidden Shapes

In this section, you are asked to find a particular shape hidden within one of the more complex figures on the right.

Straightforward questions test your ability to match a shape **exactly**, as in the example below.

More difficult questions involve the changing of one or more of the target shape's elements such as size, shading, orientation or angle. An exact match is always preferred, if possible.

Example:

In which of the figures on the right is the shape on the left hidden?

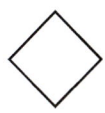

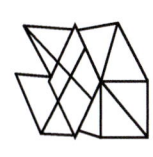

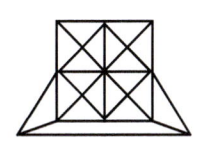

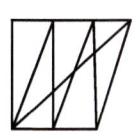

Answer: c

Explanation:

Remember, if present, an exact match is always the best answer. Otherwise, look for the option containing the target shape with minimal modification.

Narrower and taller versions of the target diamond shape can be viewed in options a and b.

Option **c**, however, contains an unchanged, exact copy, shown in purple below.

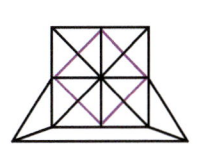

© 2018 ElevenPlusExams.co.uk   COPYING STRICTLY PROHIBITED

Hidden Shapes

In which of the figures on the right is the shape on the left hidden?

1

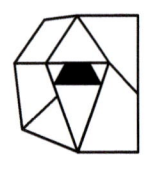

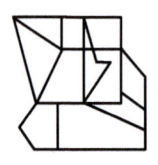

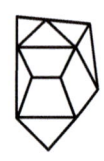

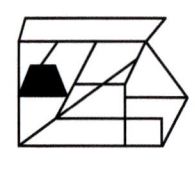

   a   b   c   d   e

2

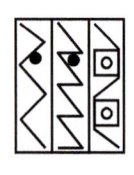

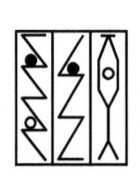

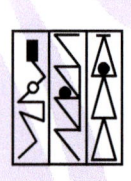

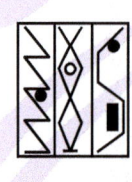

   a   b   c   d   e

3

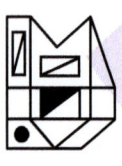

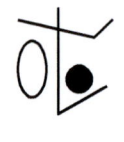

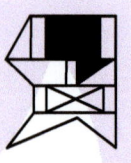

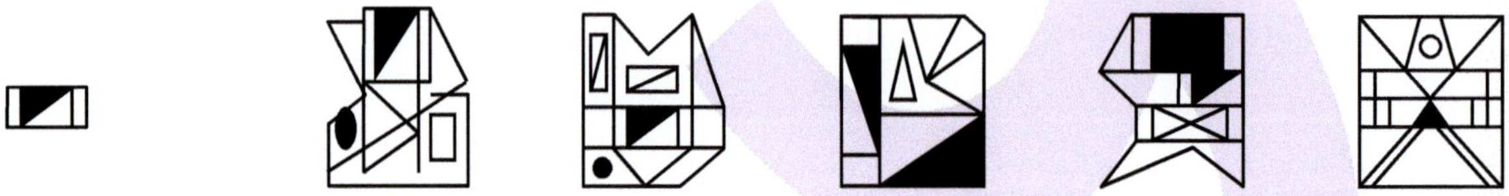

   a   b   c   d   e

4

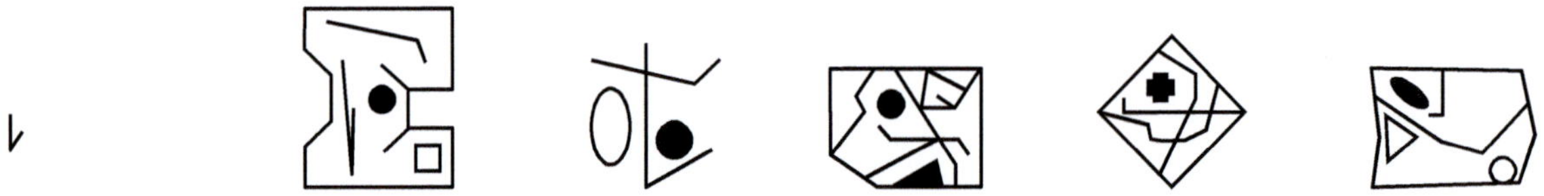

   a   b   c   d   e

© 2018 ElevenPlusExams.co.uk   COPYING STRICTLY PROHIBITED

Hidden Shapes

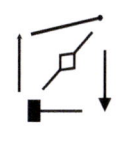

In which of the figures on the right is the shape on the left hidden?

5

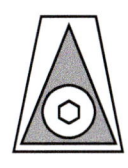

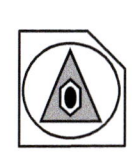

    a   b   c   d   e

6

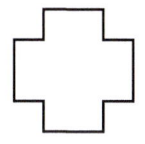

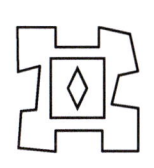

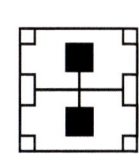

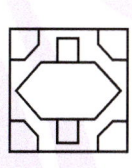

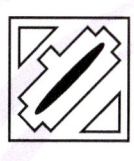

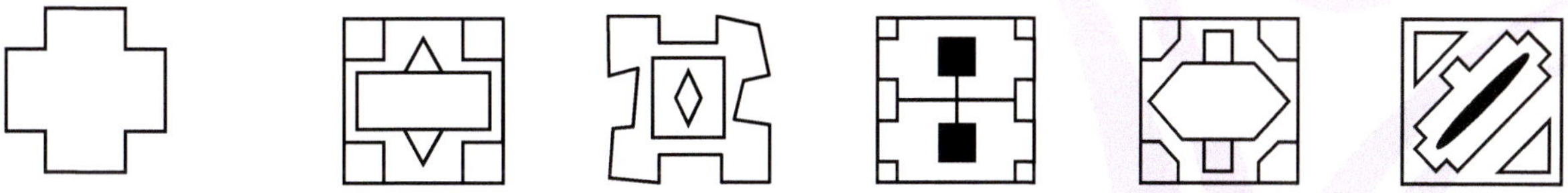

    a   b   c   d   e

7

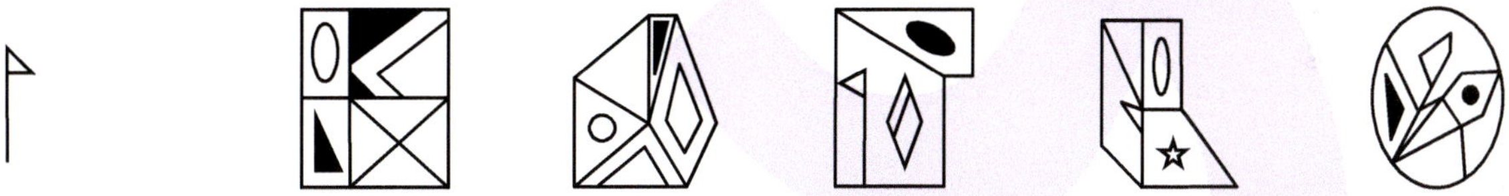

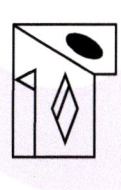

    a   b   c   d   e

8

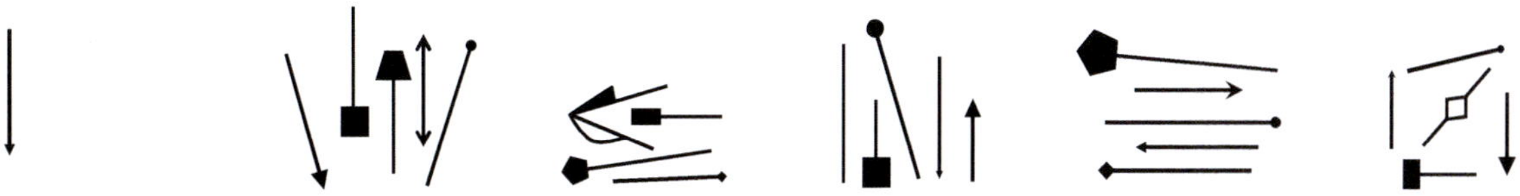

    a   b   c   d   e

Hidden Shapes

In which of the figures on the right is the shape on the left hidden?

9

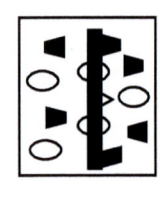

a  b  c  d  e

10

a  b  c  d  e

Identify the Pair

In this section, you are asked to find which two figures of the five options are the same.

Look for obvious element differences to eliminate certain options quickly.

Remember also that two figures can be at different angles but still be identical.

Example:

Which two figures are the same?

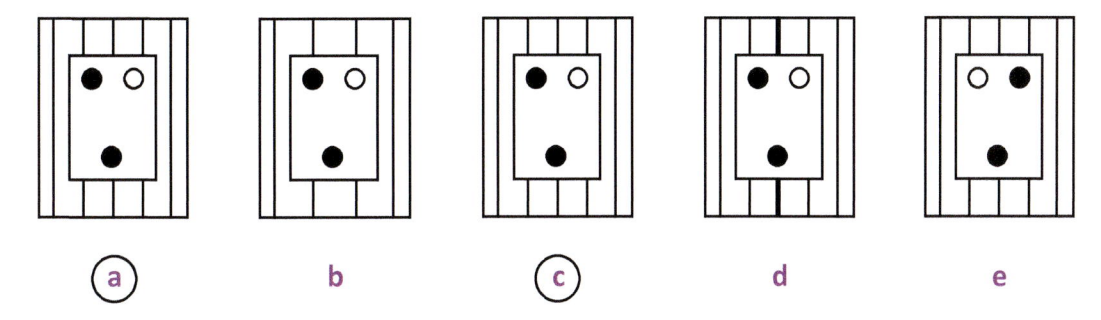

a   b   c   d   e

Answer: a & c

Explanation:

Options b, d and e can be eliminated due to an incorrect number of vertical lines in b, the wrong line thickness in d, and a different circle shading pattern in e.

Options a & c are an exact match and therefore the correct answer.

Identify the Pair

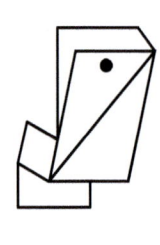

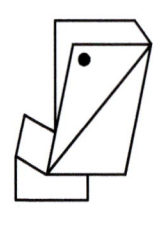

Which two figures are the same?

1

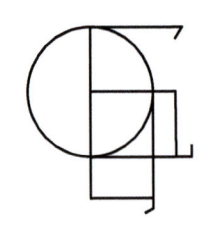

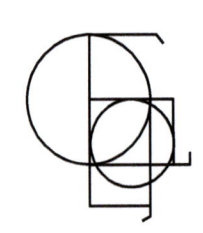

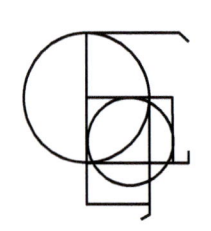

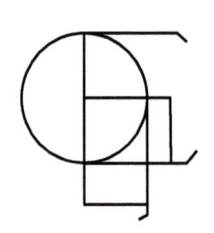

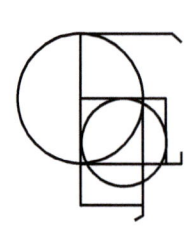

a   b   c   d   e

2

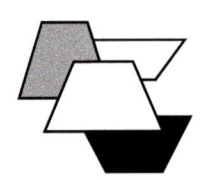

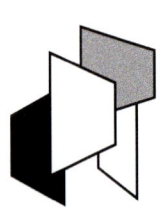

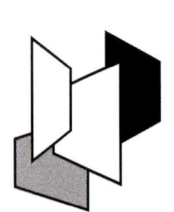

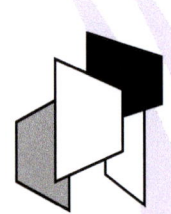

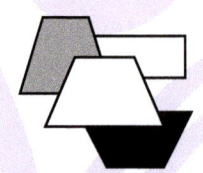

a   b   c   d   e

3

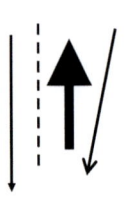

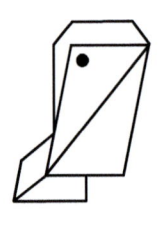

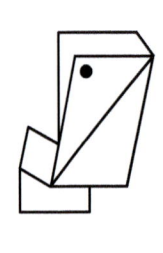

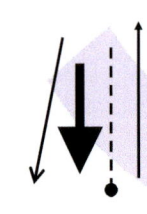

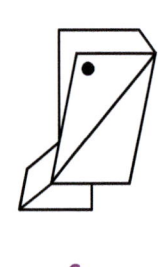

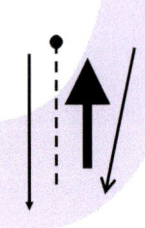

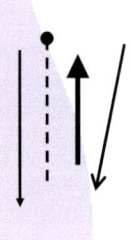

a   b   c   d   e

4

a   b   c   d   e

Identify the Pair

Which two figures are the same?

5

a b c d e

6

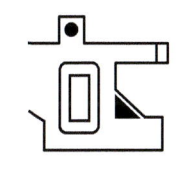

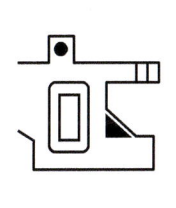

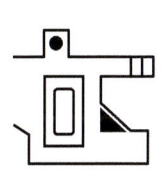

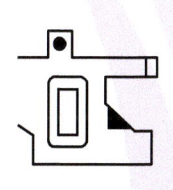

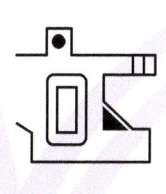

a b c d e

7

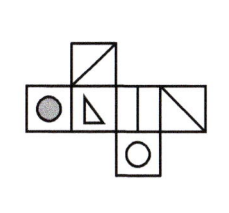

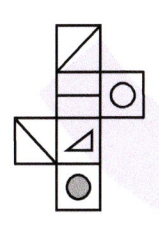

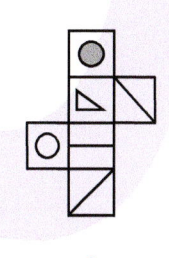

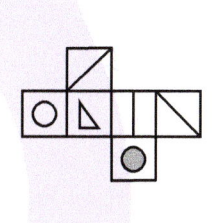

a b c d e

8

a b c d e

Identify the Pair

Which two figures are the same?

9

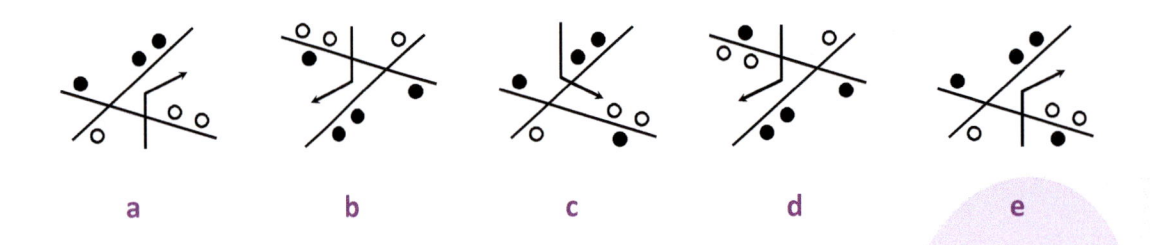

a b c d e

10

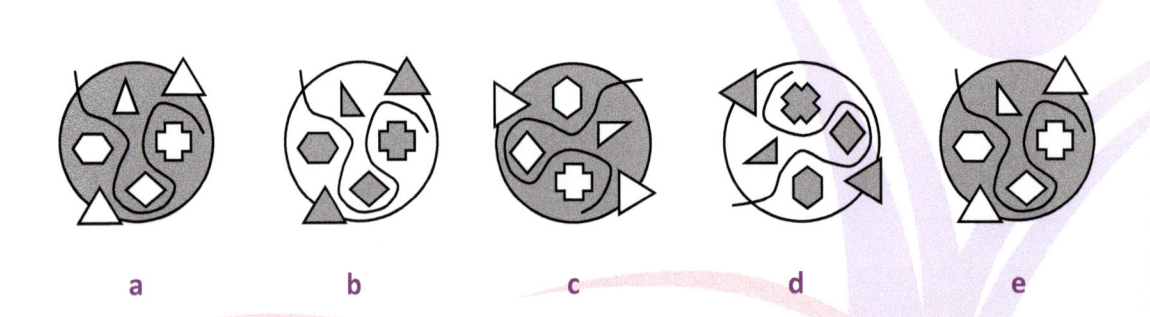

a b c d e

…

Combine the Shapes

In this section, you are asked to determine which of the shapes on the right is formed from the two shapes on the left.

Either shape on the left can be rotated, reflected or transparent, but neither can be altered in size or shading.

Example:

Which shape on the right has been formed from the two shapes on the left?

a   b   c   d   e

Answer: e

Explanation:

When the first shape is rotated through 90 degrees and placed inside the bottom of the second shape, answer **e** is produced.

Combine the Shapes

Which shape on the right has been formed from the two shapes on the left?

1

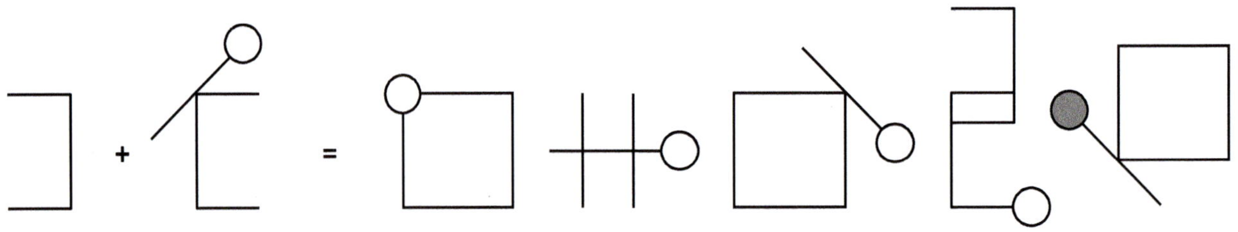

      a   b   c   d   e

2

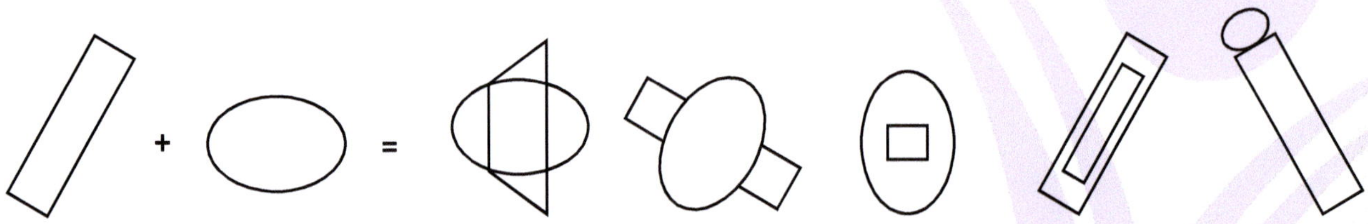

      a   b   c   d   e

3

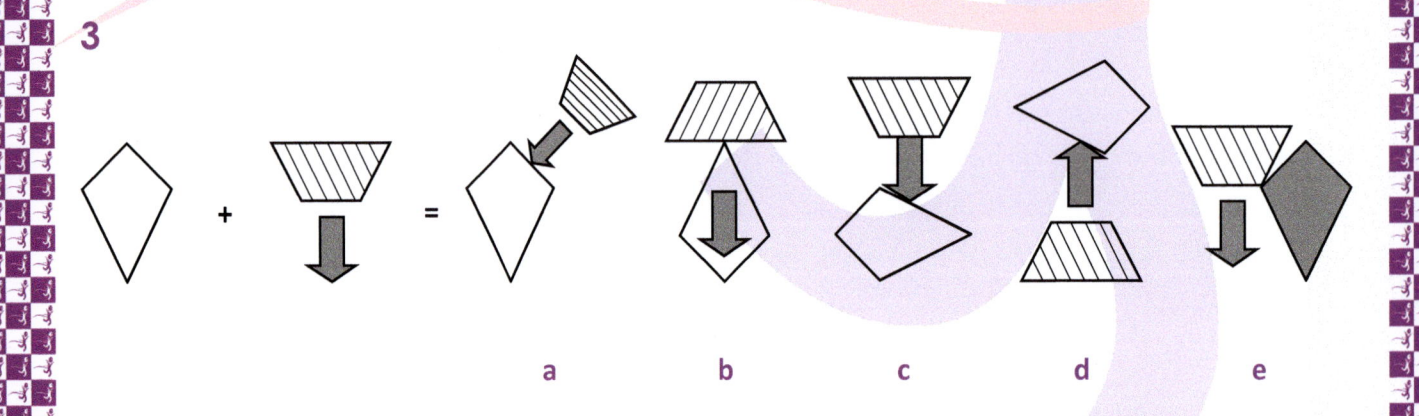

      a   b   c   d   e

4

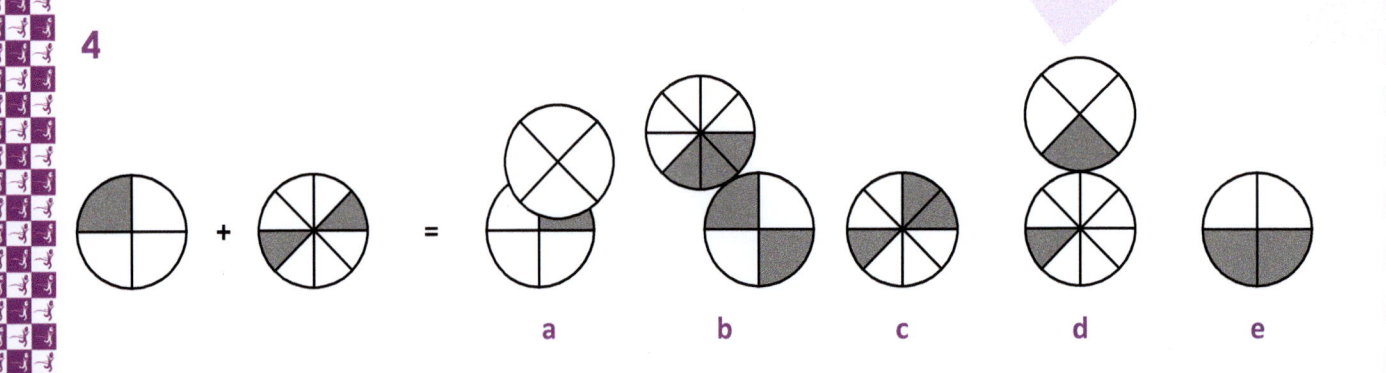

      a   b   c   d   e

Combine the Shapes

Which shape on the right has been formed from the two shapes on the left?

5

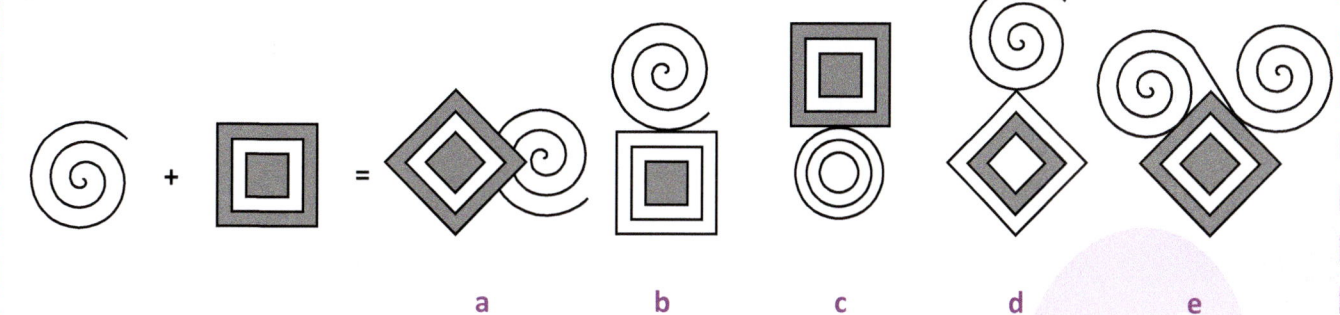

    a   b   c   d   e

6

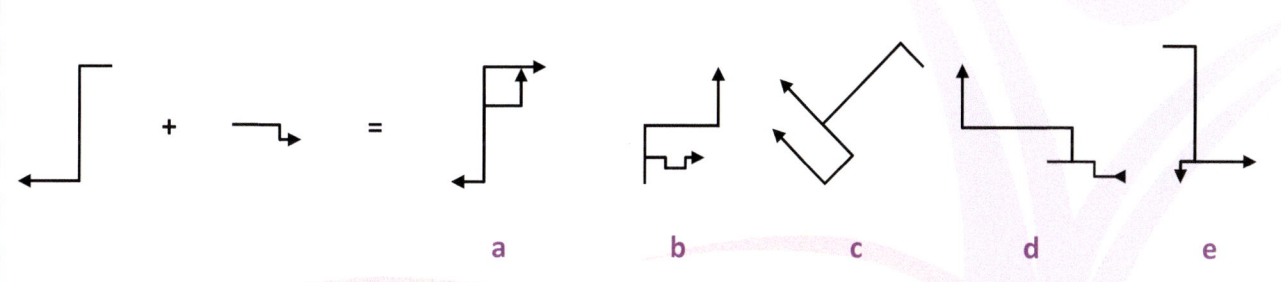

    a   b   c   d   e

7

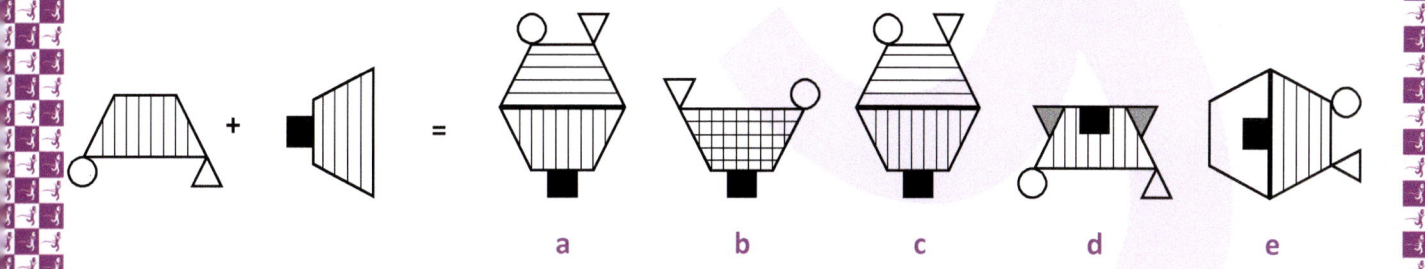

    a   b   c   d   e

8

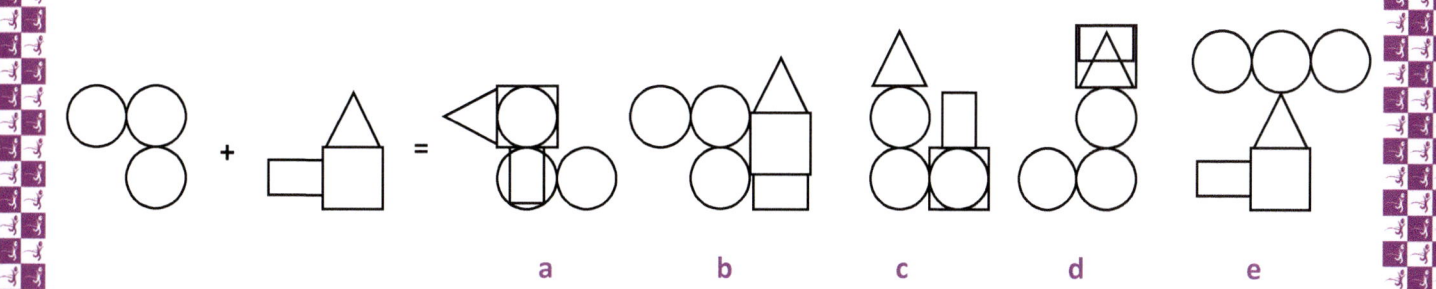

    a   b   c   d   e

Combine the Shapes

Which shape on the right has been formed from the two shapes on the left?

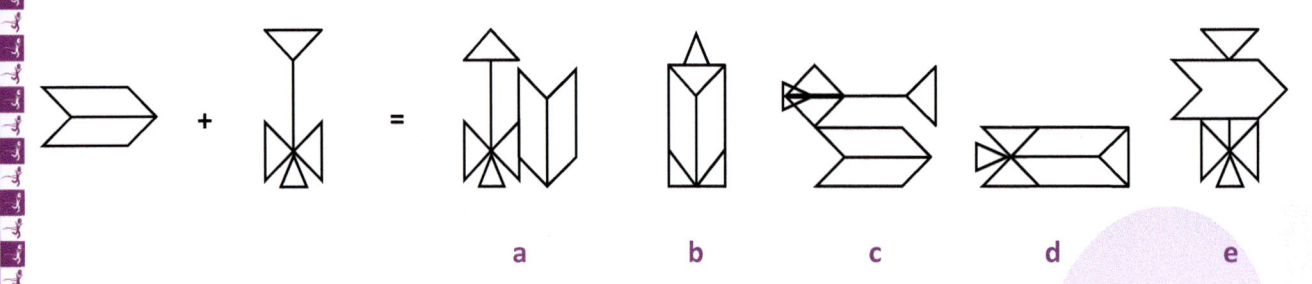

9

    a   b   c   d   e

10

    a   b   c   d   e

FIRST PAST THE POST

Rotations Analogies

In this section, you are asked to determine the degree of rotation through which the first shape in the first pair has been rotated to form the second shape in that pair. The same degree of rotation must be applied to the second pair of shapes.

The shapes only rotate in a **clockwise** direction.

Example:

Which shape on the right has been rotated through the same number of degrees as the shape on the left?

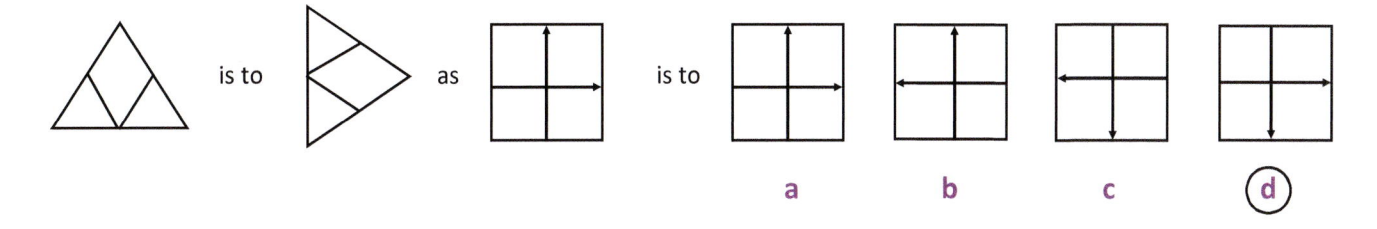

Answer: d

Explanation:

The first figure in the first pair has been rotated through 90 degrees to create the second figure.

Therefore, the first figure in the second pair must also be rotated through 90 degrees, giving figure **d**.

Rotation Analogies

Which shape on the right has been rotated through the same number of degrees as the shape on the left?

1

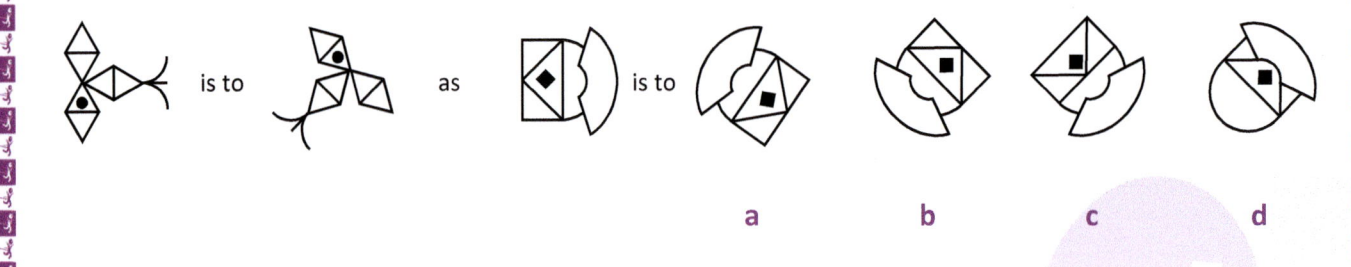

2

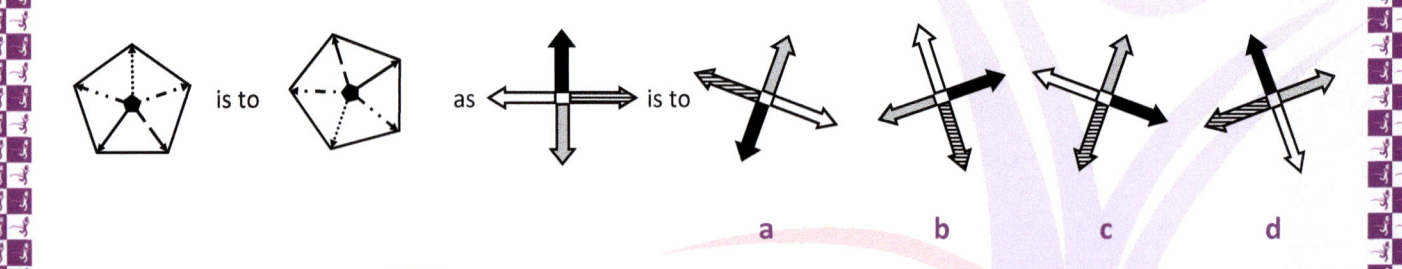

3

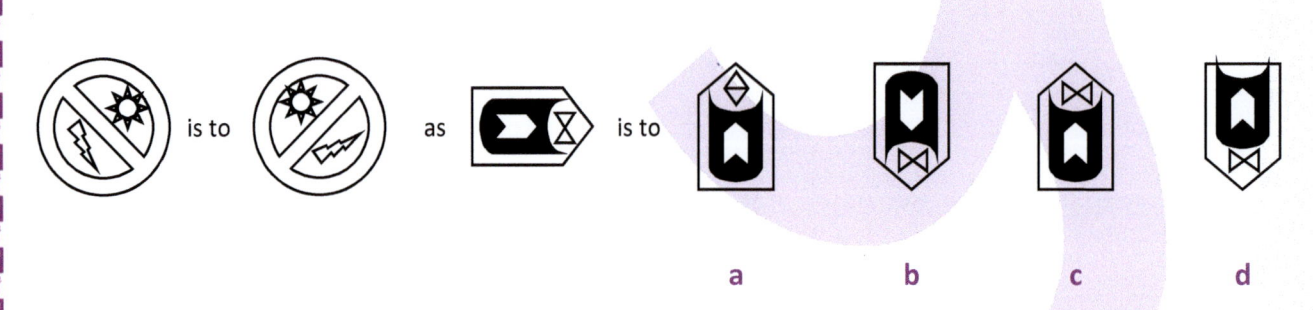

4

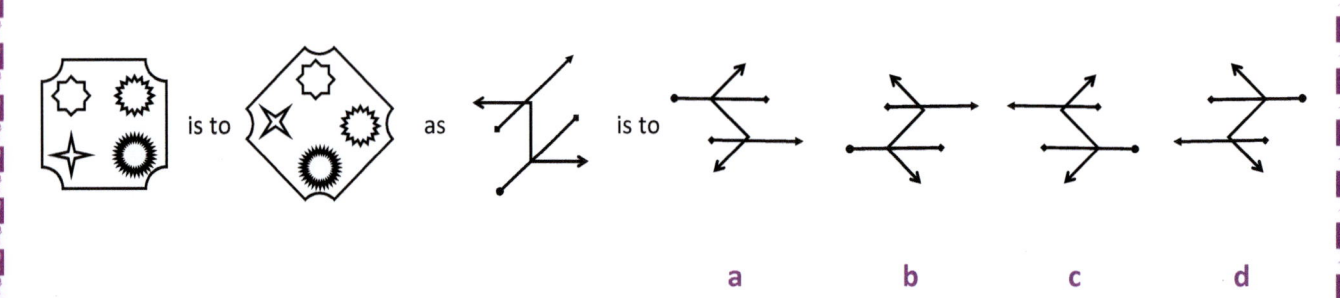

Rotation Analogies

Which shape on the right has been rotated through the same number of degrees as the shape on the left?

5

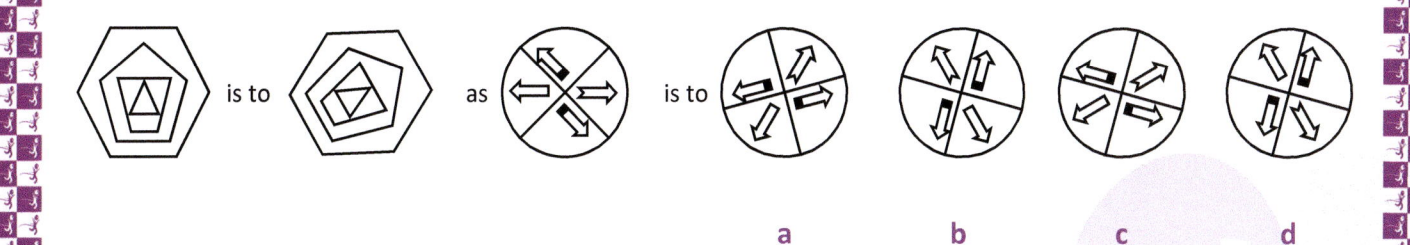

6

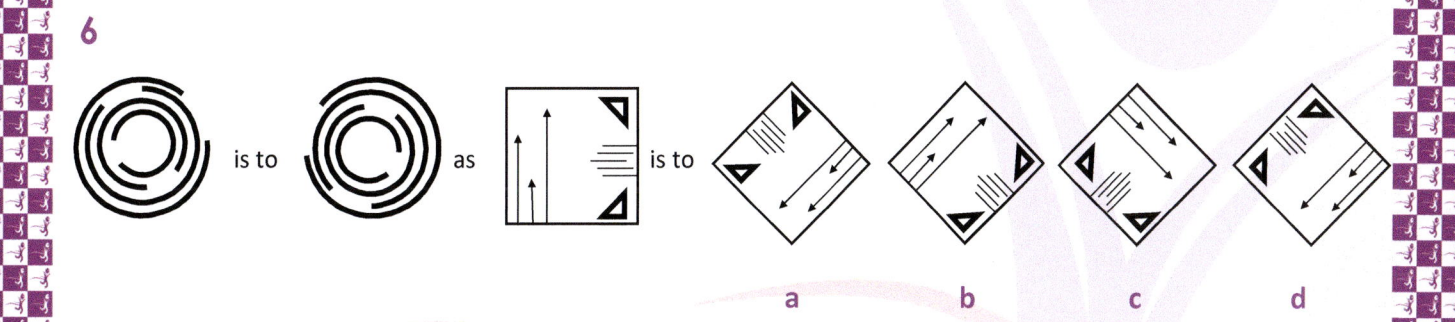

7

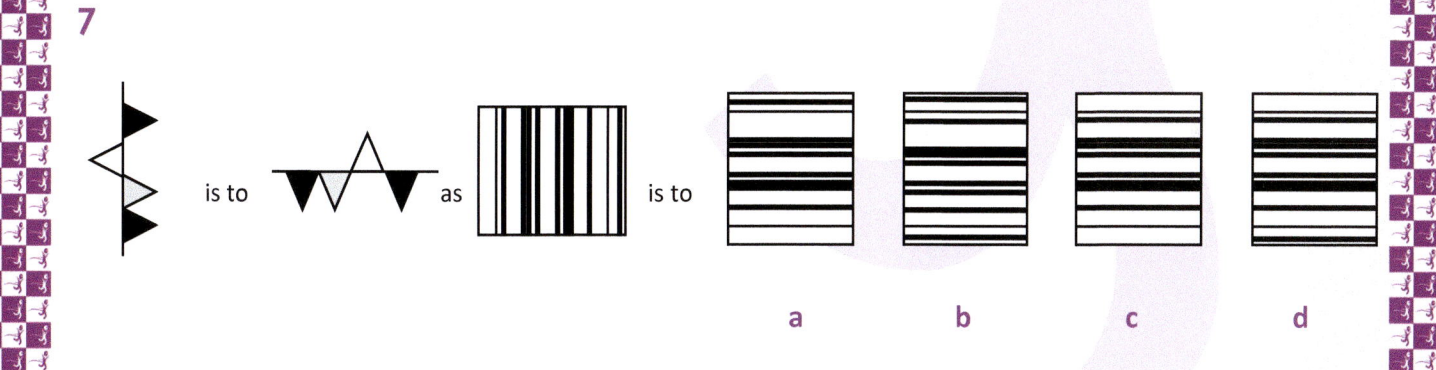

8

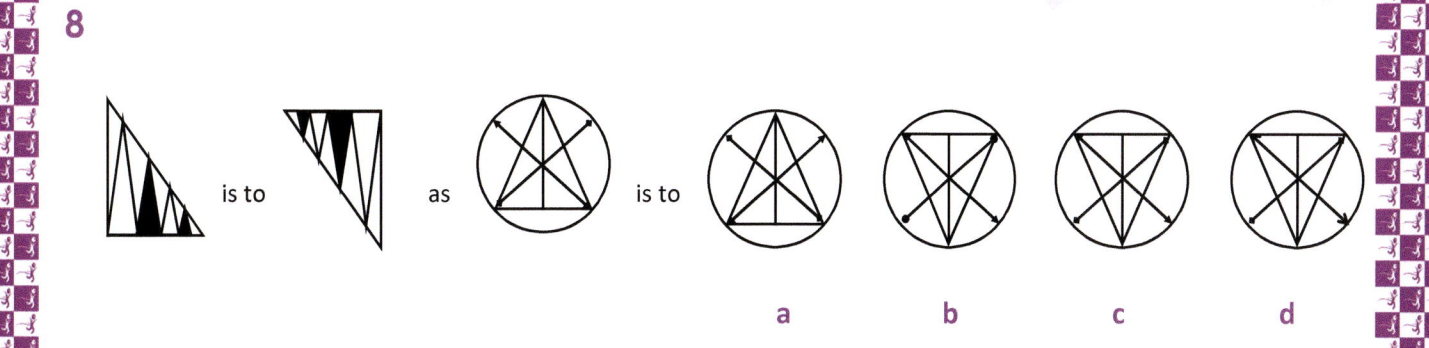

Rotation Analogies

Which shape on the right has been rotated through the same number of degrees as the shape on the left?

9

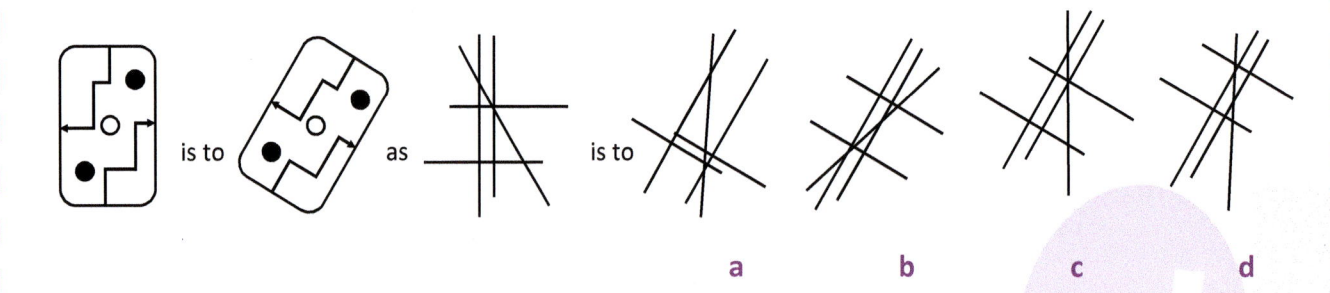

10

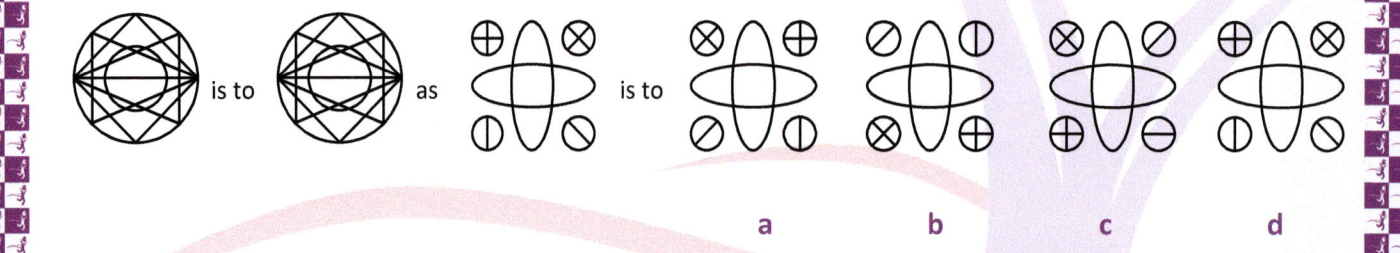

Reflection Analogies

In this section, you are asked to determine the mirror line in which the first shape in the first pair has been reflected to form the second shape in that pair. The first shape in the second pair must also be reflected in the same mirror line.

The mirror line may be horizontal, vertical or diagonal.

Example:

Which shape on the right has been reflected in the same mirror line as the shape on the left?

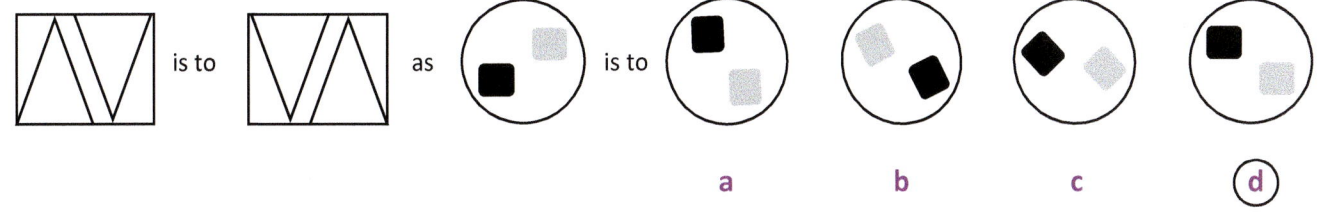

Answer: d

Explanation:

The first figure in the first pair has been reflected in an horizontal mirror line to create the second figure. Therefore, the first figure in the second pair must be reflected in an horizontal mirror line, giving figure d.

Reflection Analogies

Which shape on the right has been reflected in the same mirror line as the shape on the left?

1

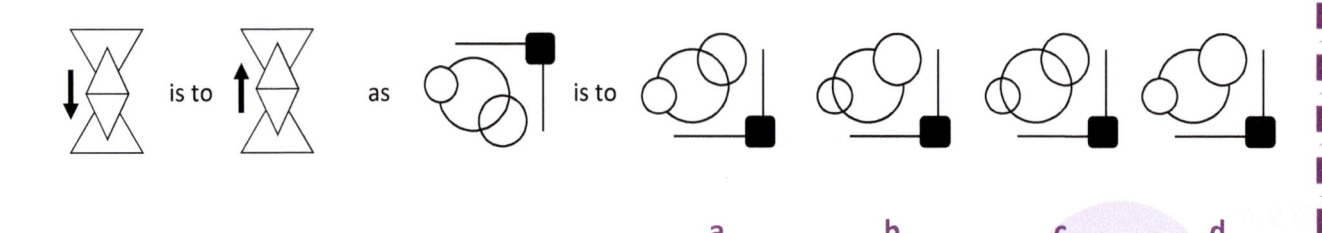

2

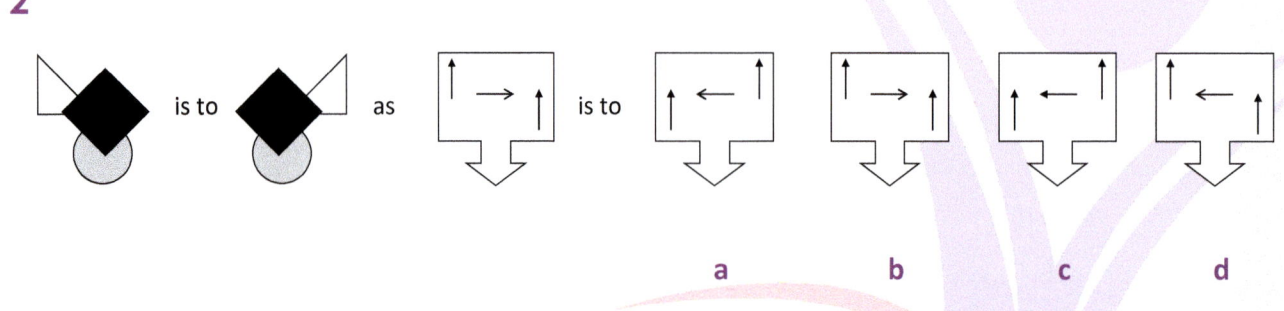

3

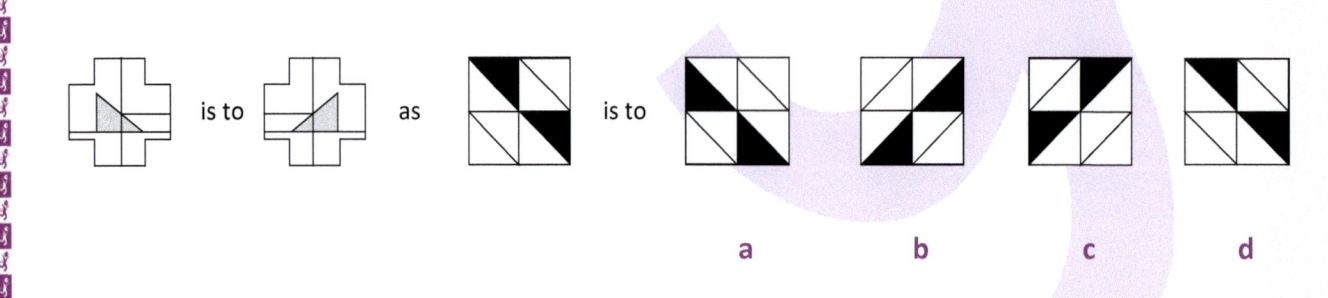

4

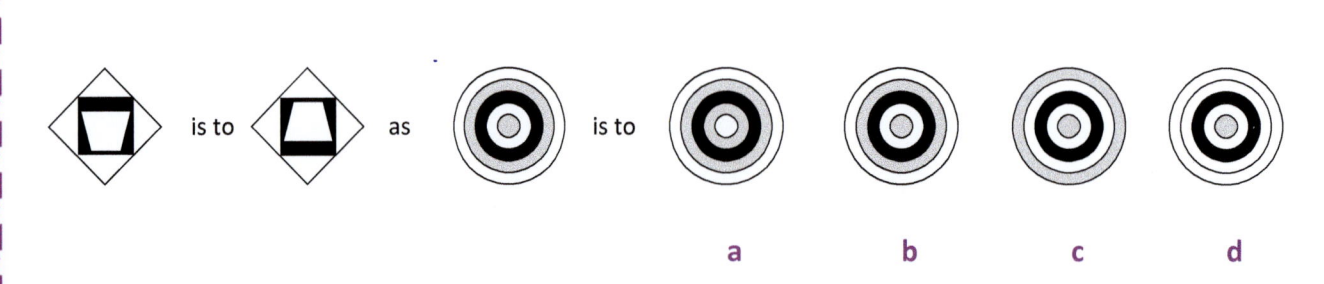

Reflection Analogies

Which shape on the right has been reflected in the same mirror line as the shape on the left?

5

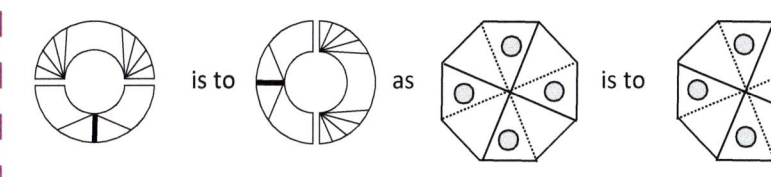

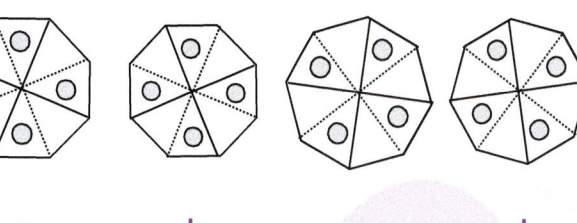

6

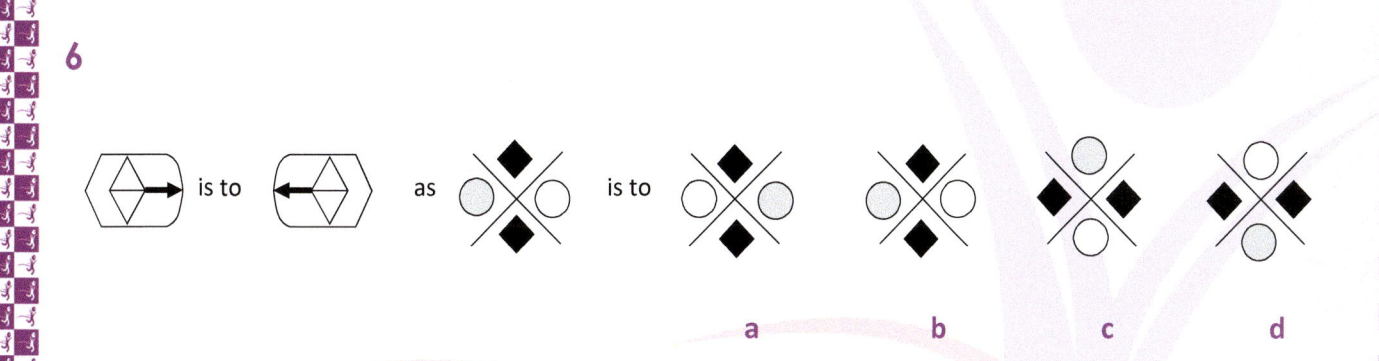

7

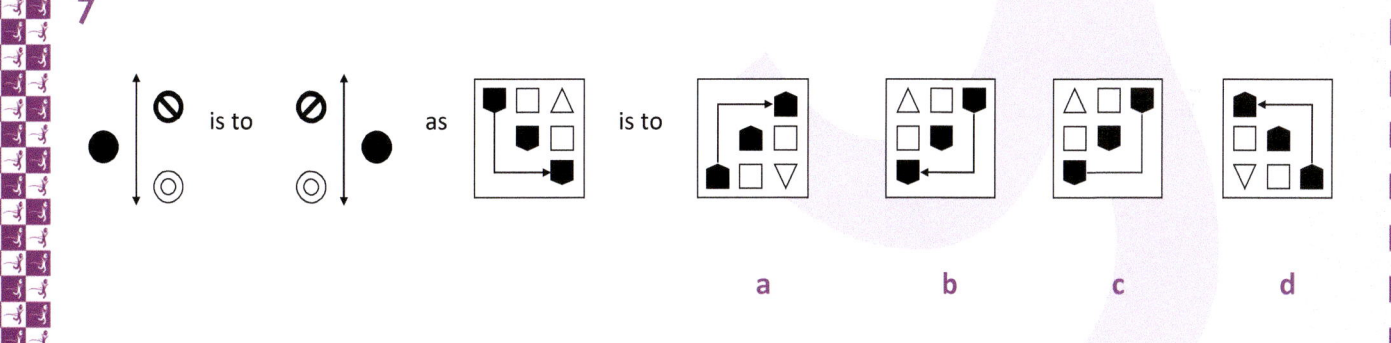

8

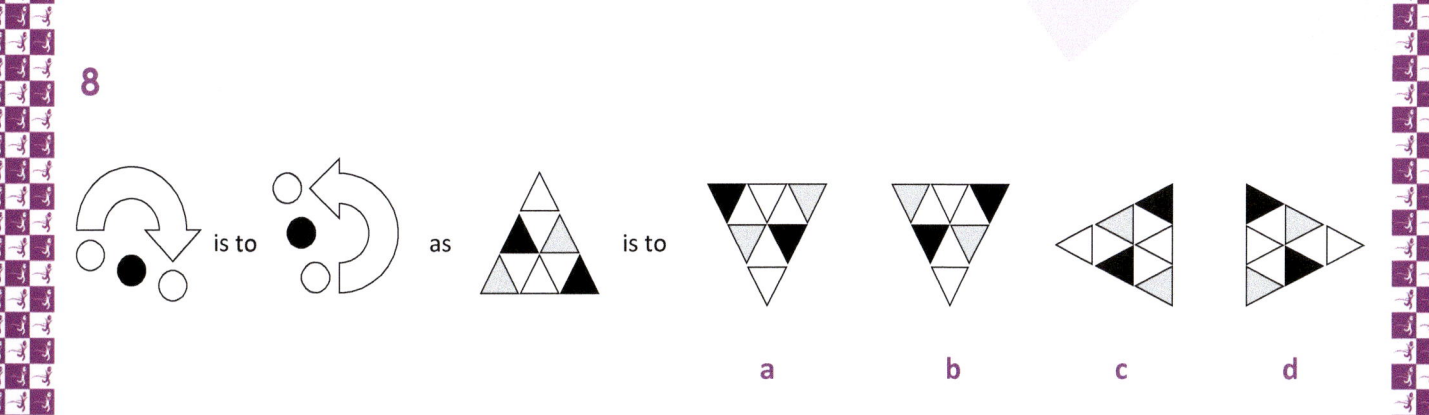

Reflection Analogies

Which shape on the right has been reflected in the same mirror line as the shape on the left?

9

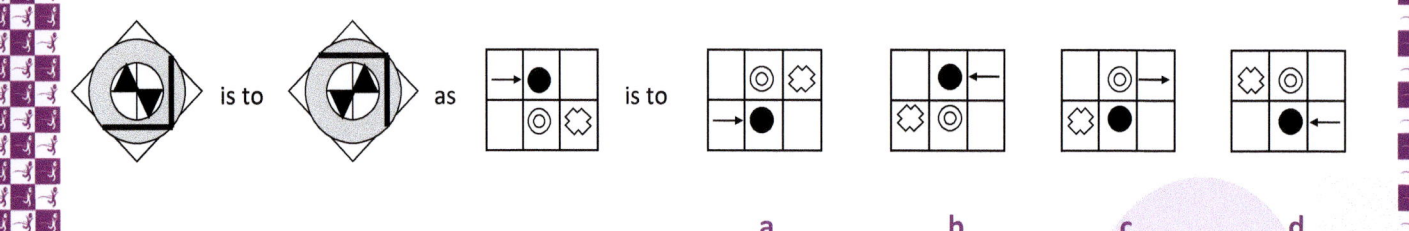

    a   b   c   d

10

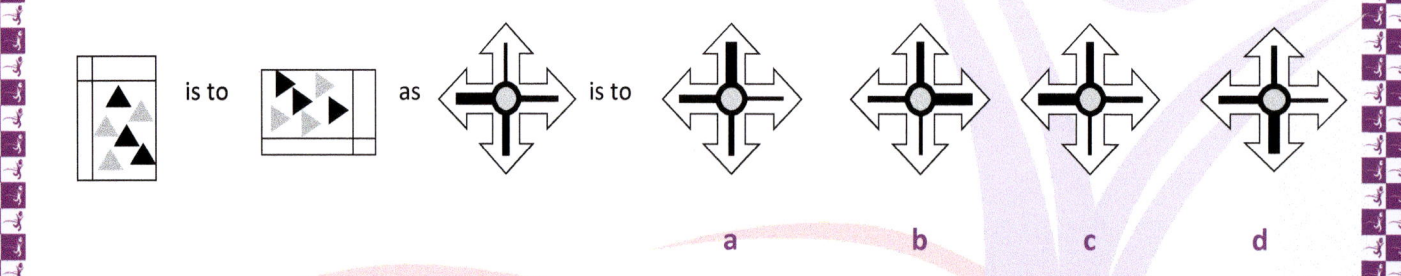

    a   b   c   d

Cross Sections

In this section, you are asked to determine which of the 2D cross sections on the right is formed when the 3D shape on the left is sliced either, horizontally or vertically, through its centre.

Straightforward questions ask the cross section of a single 3D shape, whereas more complex questions ask the cross section of a solid made up of multiple 3D shapes.

Example:

Which shape on the right is the 2D **horizontal** cross section of the centre of the 3D shape on the left?

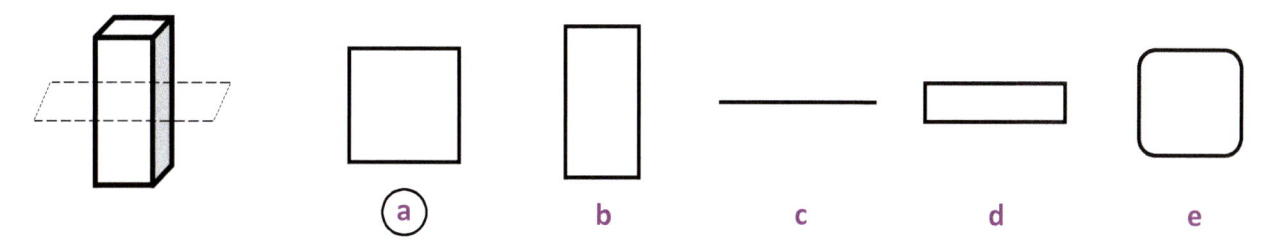

Answer: a

Explanation:

The 3D shape is a cuboid. The 2D horizontal cross section of a cuboid is either a square or rectangle. This shape has a square base, so the 2D cross section is **a**.

Cross Sections

Which shape on the right is the 2D horizontal cross section of the centre of the 3D shape on the left?

1

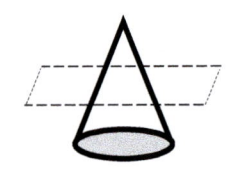

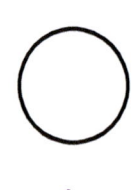

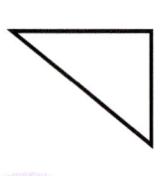

a   b   c   d   e

2

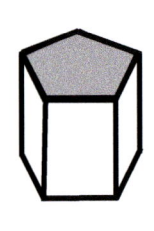

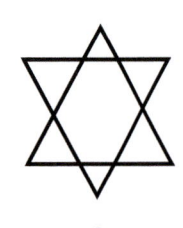

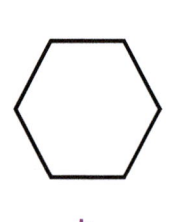

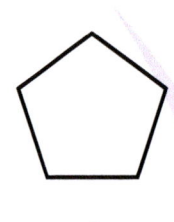

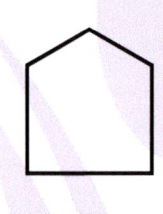

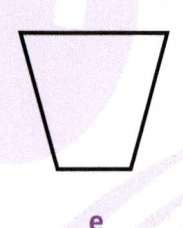

a   b   c   d   e

3

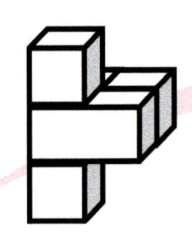

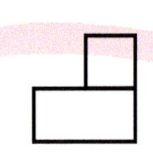

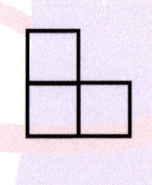

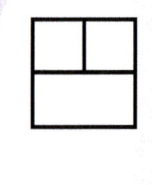

a   b   c   d   e

4

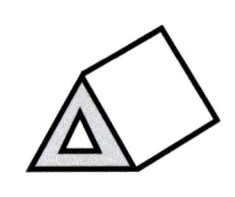

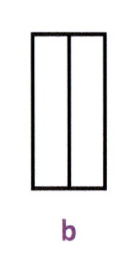

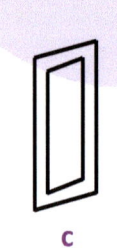

a   b   c   d   e

5

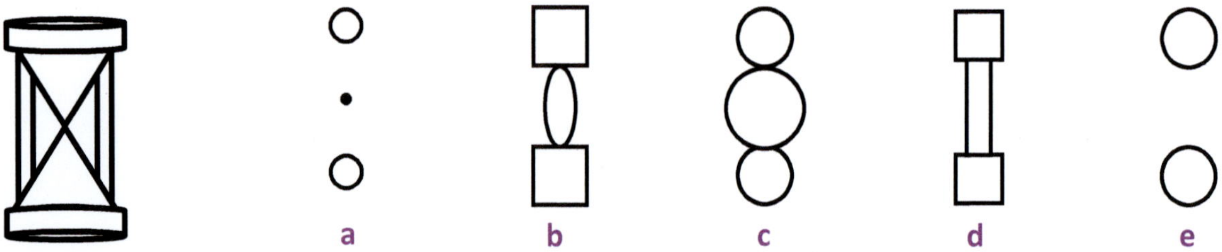

a   b   c   d   e

Cross Sections

Which shape on the right is the 2D vertical cross section of the centre of the 3D shape on the left?

6

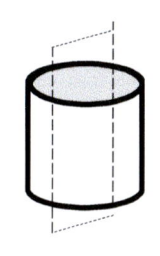

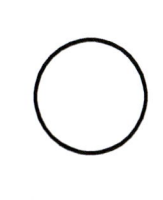

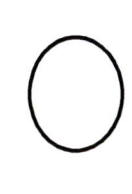

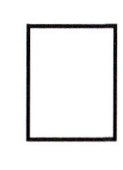

      a   b   c   d   e

7

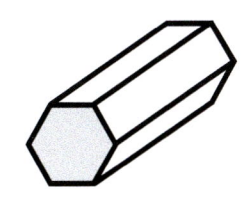

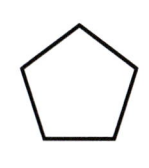

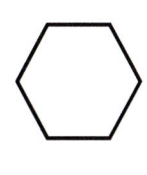

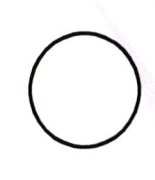

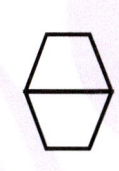

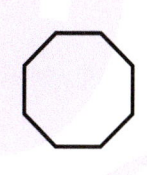

      a   b   c   d   e

8

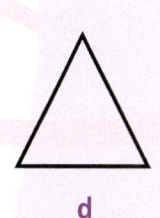

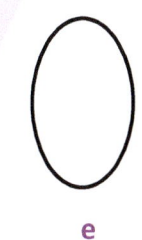

      a   b   c   d   e

9

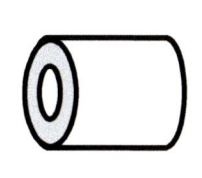

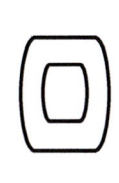

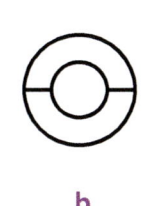

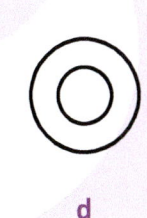

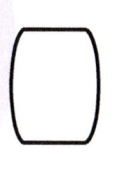

      a   b   c   d   e

10

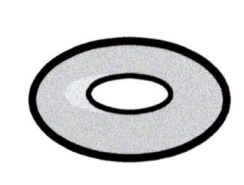

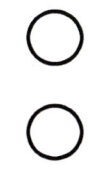

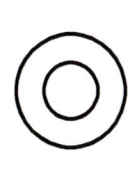

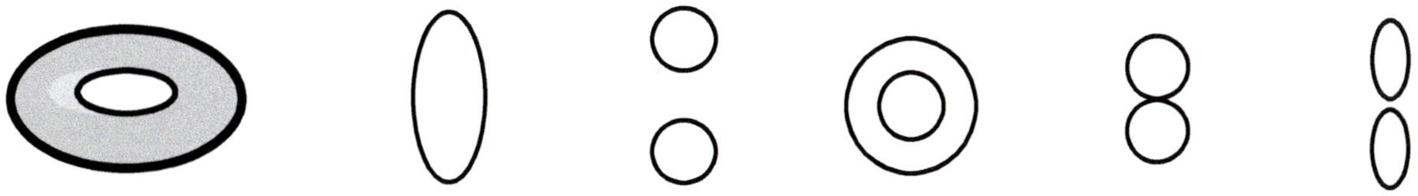

      a   b   c   d   e

BLANK PAGE

FIRST PAST THE POST

Answers & Explanations

Non-Verbal Reasoning:

2D

Multiple Choice

Book 1

Sequences, pages 1-4

Question	Answer	Explanation
1	a	At each step, the shape is being rotated 90 degrees clockwise but the shading of the large squares always remains the same. The shading of the small squares alternates from white-black-white to black-white-black. Therefore, the answer is **a**.
2	e	At each step, a half shaded circle is added to the pattern. If the previous pattern already contains a half shaded circle, that circle is replaced with one full unshaded circle and one full shaded circle. Therefore, the answer is **e**.
3	e	Each pattern consists of five shapes: a hexagon, circle, triangle, square and a cross. At each step, one of the five shapes becomes invisible and this shape changes in an anticlockwise cycle. One of the five shapes is shaded and the remaining four are unshaded. At each step, the shape which is shaded also changes, but in a clockwise cycle. Therefore, the answer is **e**.
4	c	The shape rotates anticlockwise in 90 degree steps. The circle touching the straight side of the shape starts on its right-hand side and moves towards its left-hand side, at each step. Also at each step, one of the lines within the shape moves from near the straight side of the shape towards the centre of the shape. Therefore, the answer is **c**.
5	c	In each pattern, three shapes are shown in a vertical line. All three shapes are the same in style and alternate between three hexagons and three trapeziums. The shading pattern repeats every three figures, with the position of the shaded shape moving upwards at each step. The line inside the top shape is rotated anticlockwise in 45 degree steps. Therefore, the answer is **c**.
6	a	At each step, the number of circles decreases by one while the number of crosses increases by one. Therefore, the answer is **a**.
7	b	At each step, either a small unshaded square or large shaded square is added to the pattern, alternating between being added vertically and horizontally. Therefore, the answer is **b**.
8	e	At each step, the number of hexagons increases by one and the number of hexagons which are shaded increases by one. Therefore, the answer is **e**.
9	a	The shaded circle moves down the stairs in steps of one and is always placed just above the stairs. The unshaded circle moves up the stairs in steps of one and is always just under the stairs. Therefore, the answer is **a**.
10	b	Each pattern is made up of alternating circles and short horizontal lines. At each step, the bottommost circle or line in the top section moves downwards to the bottom section. Therefore, the answer is **b**.

Analogies, pages 5-8

Question	Answer	Explanation
1	c	The top three shapes in the first figure are enlarged and put in reverse order in a vertical line to make the second figure, with the triangle now pointing in the opposite direction. Therefore, the answer is **c**.
2	e	The first and second figures in each pair contain equal numbers of smaller shapes. The first figure contains only unshaded squares and the second figure contains six-sided shapes, half of which are shaded. The outer shape is squashed. Therefore, the answer is **e**.
3	d	If the second figure in each pair is rotated 90 degrees clockwise it would connect with the first figure in each pair to form a rectangle. Therefore, the answer is **d**.
4	b	The top shape in the second figure is the same as the top face of the 3D shape in the first figure. The top shape in the second figure is connected by a short vertical line to a horizontal rectangle. Therefore, the answer is **b**.
5	e	The shape is rotated 180 degrees and the line style changes between solid and dotted or vice versa. Therefore, the answer is **e**.
6	a	Everything remains the same except the line style. The thicker horizontal lines become arrows and vice versa, therefore the circles become arrows and vice versa. Therefore, the answer is **a**.
7	d	The shape is rotated 180 degrees and the arrow styles change. One arrow style has two lines for its border, while the other has a single dotted line with a shaded arrowhead. Therefore, the answer is **d**.
8	e	The same three shapes are ordered in a vertical line with the innermost at the top and the outermost at the bottom. Therefore, the answer is **e**.
9	b	The second figure is made up of two vertical shapes: the left shape is a copy of the first figure, but the triangles or parallelograms with the circles are now empty and the empty triangle or parallelograms are now shaded. The right of the two shapes in the second figure is the first figure rotated by 180 degrees. Therefore, the answer is **b**.
10	a	The second figure is a 180 degree rotation of the first figure. Once rotated, the vertical lines inside the shape become horizontal lines and the short horizontal rectangle changes between shaded and unshaded or vice versa. Therefore, the answer is **a**.

Codes, pages 9-12

Question	Answer	Explanation
1	c	First letter = number of arcs: A (1), U (2), G (3), B (4) Second letter = number of shaded circles: S (0), R (1), E (2) Shape consists of three arcs and two shaded circles, code GE. Therefore, the answer is **c**.
2	a	First letter = shading: B (only the inner shape is shaded), P (the whole shape is shaded), T (no shading) Second letter = larger shape style: D (hexagon), R (square), S (circle), X (triangle) Shape is fully shaded and a hexagon, code PD. Therefore, the answer is **a**.
3	d	First letter = outer shape style: F (square), I (hexagon), J (circle), K (trapezium) Second letter = number and position of shaded circles: H (4), R (two in a vertical line), V (two in an horizontal line) Shape has an hexagonal outer shape and contains two circles in an horizontal line, code IV. Therefore, the answer is **d**.
4	e	First letter = number of larger squares: V (0), O (1), S (2), B (3) Second letter = position of shaded square: Y (bottom), X (middle), Z (top) Shape consists of no large squares, and the bottom of the three small squares is shaded, code VY. Therefore, the answer is **e**.
5	b	First letter = number of curved lines: V (2), L (3) Second letter = number of intersection points between lines: B (2), C (3), Z (4) Shape consists of three curved lines with three intersections, code LC. Therefore, the answer is **b**.
6	c	First letter = line direction within circle: A (left-slanting), M (vertical), W (right-slanting) Second letter = number and style of smaller shapes: B (one square), F (one circle), Q (one triangle), L (one circle and one square) Shape has a left slanting line within the circle and one small square, code AB. Therefore, the answer is **c**
7	d	First letter = size and shading of square: M (small and unshaded), O (small and shaded), W (large and unshaded) Second letter = number of circles: C (2), E (3), X (4), F (5) Shape consists of a small unshaded square and five circles, code MF. Therefore, the answer is **d**.
8	e	First letter = number of small circles: Q (1), P (2), A (3), E (4) Second letter = number of small shaded circles: N (0), K (1), O (2) Shape has three small circles, one of which is shaded, code AK. Therefore, the answer is **e**.
9	a	First letter = position of two thicker lines: B (perpendicular), E (horizontal), R (vertical), Y (slanting) Second letter = number of intersection points between thicker and thinner lines: I (1), D (2), W (3) Shape has two horizontal thicker lines and three intersection points, code EW. Therefore, the answer is **a**.
10	a	First letter = contents of four squares immediately adjacent to the centre square: C (all are shaded), F (all contain circles), H (all contain crosses) Second letter = contents of centre square: B (a cross), O (a circle), R (a line), Z (shaded) Shape consists of four shaded squares adjacent to the centre square, which contains a cross, code CB. Therefore, the answer is **a**.

Similarities, pages 13-16

Question	Answer	Explanation
1	c	The shapes consist only of straight-edged squares. Therefore, the answer is **c**.
2	e	Each figure consists of one circle and one hexagon which interlink. The size of the circle and hexagon can vary. Therefore, the answer is **e**.
3	b	Each figure is an image of a stick person with two straight lines for arms and two straight lines for legs. The head consists of an empty circle. Therefore, the answer is **b**.
4	e	One end of the line has a shaded triangle. The other end has a shaded or unshaded shape. The smaller angle between the two lines is obtuse. Therefore, the answer is **e**.
5	a	Each figure consists of three identical shapes, which all touch and are arranged in a triangular formation with one shape in the top row and two shapes in the bottom row. At least one of the three shapes must be shaded. Therefore, the answer is **a**.
6	d	Each figure consists of a square, rectangle, circle and triangle. Each shape must touch at least one other shape. None of the shapes interlink or lie inside another shape. Therefore, the answer is **d**.
7	c	Each figure consists of a straight line with a shape on both ends. If the two shapes are the same, one is shaded and one is unshaded. If the shapes are different, they are both shaded. Therefore, the answer is **c**.
8	b	Each figure consists of an unshaded larger shape with a smaller version of the shape inside it. The smaller shape must touch an edge of the larger shape but not cross it. The smaller shape can be shaded or unshaded. Therefore, the answer is **b**.
9	b	The number of sides on each shape with curved lines attached is one less than the total number of sides on the shape. The curved lines do not enter the main shape. Therefore, the answer is **b**.
10	e	Each figure consists of a pentagon with a set of smaller shapes inside it. The figures are identical but have been rotated. The unshaded triangle in the centre must always point to the diamond in one corner, which contains a shaded small circle. The bottom left corner of the unshaded triangle points towards a corner of the pentagon with a dotted line. The bottom right corner of the unshaded triangle points towards the corner of the pentagon with a curved line. Therefore, the answer is **e**.

Odd One Out, pages 17-20

Question	Answer	Explanation
1	a	In all figures but **a**, the arrows are either horizontal or vertical.
2	d	In all figures but **d**, there is at least one right angle.
3	c	In all figures but **c**, the shaded circles are linked together, one after the other, by a single line with two ends.
4	b	In all figures but **b**, the front-to-back order of shading is unshaded, grey-shaded and dark-shaded.
5	a	In all figures but **a**, the line intersects the circle twice.
6	c	In all figures but **c**, the number of sides on the inner shape is one less than the number of sides on the outer shape.
7	a	Figure **a** is the only six-sided shape that is unshaded.
8	d	Each figure is made up of a large shape and a small shape of the same style. The position of the arrow through the large shape is reflected to give the position of the dotted line through the small shape. In figure **d**, the dotted line is in the wrong position.
9	c	In all figures but **c**, there are grey-shaded hearts.
10	a	In all figures but **a**, the arrow points towards the right.

Complete the Square Grid, pages 21-24

Question	Answer	Explanation
1	d	Going downwards, the squares in each column contain the same shapes, but have been rotated 90 degrees clockwise. Each column contains one shape which is unshaded, one shape which is shaded grey and one shape with a parallel line shading. Therefore, the answer is **d**.
2	a	The shapes in each square create a mirror image of the shapes in the squares that are vertically and horizontally adjacent to it. Therefore, the answer is **a**.
3	e	Each figure in the three squares of each row contain the same four shapes, but one of the four shapes is always invisible. The shape which is invisible in the middle row cycles round in an anticlockwise pattern. In the first and third columns, the shapes at the top of each square are shaded and the shapes at the bottom of each square are unshaded. The opposite shading pattern occurs in the second column. Therefore, the answer is **e**.
4	b	The small shaded circle in each square in the first column is shown larger and unshaded in each adjacent square in the second column. The number of short straight lines in each square of the second column is equal to the number of sides on the unshaded shape in the adjacent square of the first column. Therefore, the answer is **b**.
5	b	Each figure in the three squares of each column contain the same three shapes, but the shapes decrease in size down the column. The shape at the bottom of each row becomes the shape at the top of the next row and the remaining two shapes move down one position. Therefore, the answer is **b**.
6	c	In each row, the figure in the left column and the figure in the right column are identical. Therefore, the answer is **c**.
7	a	The shapes in the right column squares are a mirror image of the shapes in the left column squares. Therefore, the answer is **a**.
8	d	The shapes in each row are identical in style, but the number of sections within each shape either increases or decreases by two along the row. Therefore, the answer is **d**.
9	e	Each square contains an horizontal line and a larger image which exchange positions across the row. Therefore, the answer is **e**.
10	b	Looking across each row, the figures have been rotated 45 degrees clockwise. The number of small circles touching the larger shape increases by one at each stage across the row. Therefore, the answer is **b**.

Complete the Grid, pages 25-28

Question	Answer	Explanation
1	c	The shapes in the hexagons within the outer ring of the grid alternate between a circle and square. For hexagons directly opposite each other, the perpendicular lines within each shape have identical line styles, but are at 45 degrees to each other. Therefore, the answer is **c**.
2	a	The shape in each trapezium is identical in style to the corresponding parallel shape within the central square but has been inverted. Therefore, the answer is **a**.
3	d	The shapes within hexagons directly opposite each other in the grid are identical in style, but have been inverted and altered in size. Shapes are identically shaded within pairs of hexagons around the grid. Therefore, the answer is **d**.
4	c	The shapes in each triangle, when joined together, form a shape in the central cross. Therefore, the answer is **c**.
5	d	Every other hexagon around the grid contains two interlinked shapes made up of those in adjacent outer hexagons. Therefore, the answer is **d**.
6	d	Moving in an anticlockwise direction from the top right hexagon, an additional parallel line is added to each hexagon and the lines are rotated 60 degrees anticlockwise at each stage. Therefore, the answer is **d**.
7	d	Moving in a clockwise direction, the octagon rotates 90 degrees anticlockwise. Therefore, the answer is **d**.
8	c	The shapes within hexagons directly opposite each other in the grid are identical in style, but have been inverted. Therefore, the answer is **c**.
9	b	Each trapezium is split into two sections. The contents and shading of each section is identical to the nearest section in the adjacent trapezium. Therefore, the answer is **b**.
10	a	The bottom three hexagons are a vertical reflection of the top three hexagons. Therefore, the answer is **a**.

Reflections, pages 29-32

Question	Answer	Explanation
1	a	The right-leaning bubble cloud formation will appear left-leaning in the reflection, as in options a and b. The cloud in option b has been wrongly rotated. Therefore, the answer is **a**.
2	b	The left-leaning lines will appear right-leaning in the reflection as in options b and c. The dark-shaded line in option c has been lengthened. Therefore, the answer is **b**.
3	d	The left-leaning arrow will appear right-leaning in the reflection, with the arrowhead pointing downwards. Therefore, the answer is **d**.
4	c	Although options a, c and d have the required reflection angle, option a has a small shape missing and option d has a smaller oval. Therefore, the answer is **c**.
5	c	The right-leaning shape will appear left-leaning in the reflection. Therefore, the answer is **c**.
6	b	Although options a, b and c are correctly reflected in the mirror line, the shaded circle in option a is in the wrong position, and the groove in option c is not deep enough. Therefore, the answer is **b**.
7	d	The thunderbolt has been correctly reflected in options b and d. The curved shape in option b has been incorrectly rotated. Therefore, the answer is **d**.
8	d	Options c and d show the correct reflection, but the shaded circle in option c is in the incorrect position. Therefore, the answer is **d**.
9	a	The right-facing shape is shown facing left in options a, b and c. The oval shape in option b and the diamond in option c have been positioned incorrectly. Therefore, the answer is **a**.
10	d	The left-leaning shape will appear right-leaning as in options b and d. The jagged line in option b has been elongated. Therefore, the answer is **d**.

Rotations, pages 33-36

Question	Answer	Explanation
1	a	Options b and c: The circle is in the wrong position. Option d: The circle is shaded. Option **a**: Correct anticlockwise rotation through an obtuse angle.
2	b	Option a: The shading pattern of the small square has changed. Options c and d: Only the small squares have been rotated. Option **b**: Correct rotation through 180 degrees.
3	c	Options a, b and d: The shape has been changed. Option **c**: Correct rotation through 360 degrees.
4	b	Option a: The inner shapes have moved to a different position. Option c: Two of the three circles have been reduced in size. Option d: One circle is missing. Option **b**: Correct rotation through 180 degrees.
5	a	Option b: The shapes in the centre row have changed. Option c: The shapes in the centre row have changed shape and shading pattern. Option d: The shapes in the first two rows have been swapped and the shape is reflected. Option **a**: Correct clockwise rotation through 90 degrees.
6	d	Option a: The central square has changed to a circle. Option b: The arrow has not been rotated. Option c: The arrow points inwards instead of outwards. Option **d**: Correct anticlockwise rotation through 45 degrees.
7	c	Option a: The triangular shape end is flipped round. Option b: The shading pattern of the small squares is swapped. Option d: This is a rotation of the original figure's reflection. Option **c**: Correct clockwise rotation through an obtuse angle.
8	a	Option b: The shaded triangle is facing left instead of down. Option c: The stepped line is not rotated. Option d: The curved line is in the wrong position. Option **a**: Correct rotation through 180 degrees.
9	d	Option a: The shading pattern of the shapes on the end of the line is swapped. Option b: The 'D' shape is reversed. Option c: The circle is in a different position. Option **d**: Correct clockwise rotation through 45 degrees.
10	b	Option a: The small vertical lines within the larger rectangle are in a different pattern. Option c: The diagonal line is in a small square. Option d: The shaded ovals in the circles are on the wrong side. Option **b**: Correct clockwise rotation through 45 degrees.

Hidden Shapes, pages 37-40

Question	Answer	Explanation
1	e	The target shape is an irregular trapezium with two 90 degree corner angles and one vertical side. Although all five option figures contain irregular or regular trapeziums, only option e shows an exact unchanged replica of the target shape. Therefore, the answer is **e**.
2	b	Although the main outline of the target shape is repeated in options a and d, the shaded circle is in the wrong position. Option c has an unshaded circle. Options b and e show the target shape after a 180 degree rotation. Option e has an incorrectly positioned shaded circle, therefore, the answer is **b**.
3	b	The whole target shape can be seen in options a, b and c. In options a and c, however, the target shape has been stretched, leaving option b as the best answer as it is an exact match. Therefore, the answer is **b**.
4	c	Options a, b, d and e have enlarged versions of the target shape and an incorrect angle between the two line segments. In the top right corner of option c, an exact replica of the target shape can be viewed but at 90 degrees anticlockwise to the original. Therefore, the answer is **c**.
5	d	The target shape looks similar to a shaded rectangular shape with a chamfer on the top right corner, creating a shape with three right angles and five sides in total. Shapes with five sides can be seen in options d and e, but the one in e has no right angles. Option d is an unshaded, enlarged view of the target shape and is therefore the best answer. Therefore, the answer is **d**.
6	a	Two compressed versions of the target cross shape can be observed in option c. Shapes similar to the cross, but with distinct modifications to their outline, also exist in options d and e. Option a, however, contains an exact replica of the target shape and is therefore the best answer. Therefore, the answer is **a**.
7	a	The target shape is a right-angled triangle on the end of a line. Option figures c and d each contain a similar looking shape, but both have the wrong type of triangle and a different length of line. Option a shows an exact copy of the target shape, but with the triangle shaded. Therefore, the answer is **a**.
8	d	Lines with arrowheads are shown in options a, c, d and e. However, only in option d is the line length and, arrowhead size a match with the target shape. Note that the arrow has been rotated 90 degrees clockwise. Therefore, the answer is **d**.
9	c	Four of the options contain a shape resembling the target, but with an portant change to at least one minor shape within it. An exact replica of the target shape can be found in option c, but is shown as a mirror image. Therefore, the answer is **c**.
10	c	Although options b and e contain two of the three shaded rectangles in the correct size and position, only option c shows an exact copy of the complete target shape. Therefore, the answer is **c**.

Identify the Pair, pages 41-44

Question	Answer	Explanation
1	**c & e**	Option a can be eliminated because the small line at the end of the top longer line bends the wrong way. Option d can be eliminated because the small line at the end of the middle longer line bends the wrong way. Option b can be eliminated because the top line is too short. This leaves options **c** & **e** as the pair.
2	**a & b**	Option c can be eliminated because the smaller, white trapezium is on the top instead of the larger, white trapezium. Option e can be eliminated because the backmost, white trapezium is a rectangle. Option d can be eliminated because the shading pattern of the black and grey shapes is swapped round. This leaves options **a** & **b** as the pair.
3	**b & d**	Option a can be eliminated because the dotted line has no black dot at the end. Option e can be eliminated because the thicker arrow is too thin. Option c can be eliminated because the thinner arrow is pointing the wrong way. This leaves options **b** & **d** as the pair.
4	**b & e**	Option a can be eliminated because the top left corner is the wrong shape. Option c can be eliminated because the bottom left corner is the wrong shape. Option d can be eliminated because the small, black circle is too far to the right. This leaves options **b** & **e** as the pair.
5	**d & e**	Option b can be eliminated because the rectangle and the small, black circle are touching. Option a can be eliminated because the diamond is black. Option c can be eliminated because the lines within the larger circle are incorrectly oriented. This leaves options **d** & **e** as the pair.
6	**b & e**	Option d can be eliminated because the small, black triangle is touching the edge of the larger shape. Option a can be eliminated because there is only one line within the larger shape in the top right corner. Option c can be eliminated because the outer rectangle has sharp corners and the inner rectangle has rounded corners. This leaves options **b** & **e** as the pair.
7	**a & c**	Option e can be eliminated because the shading pattern of the two small circles is swapped round. Option d can be eliminated because the right-angled triangle is facing the wrong way. Option b can be eliminated because the slanting line in the right-hand square is slanting in the wrong direction. This leaves options **a** & **c** as the pair.
8	**a & e**	Option d can be eliminated because the small, vertical rectangle does not touch the base of the larger rectangle. Option c can be eliminated because the bottom corners of the trapezium do not hang over the edges of the larger rectangle. Option b can be eliminated because the small, vertical rectangle is on the wrong side. This leaves options **a** & **e** as the pair.
9	**d & e**	Option c can be eliminated because the arrow is upside down. Option a can be eliminated because the small, black circle beneath the lower line is missing. Option b can be eliminated because the three circles above the arrowhead are incorrectly positioned and shaded. This leaves options **d** & **e** as the pair.
10	**c & e**	Option a can be eliminated because it contains an isosceles triangle instead of a right-angled triangle. Option d can be eliminated because the cross shape is incorrectly oriented. Option b can be eliminated because the shading pattern is reversed. This leaves options **c** & **e** as the pair.

Combine the Shapes, pages 45-48

Question	Answer	Explanation
1	c	The square is formed when the first shape is joined to the right side of the second shape. The combined shape is then rotated 90 degrees clockwise to give option **c**.
2	b	If the second shape is rotated 60 degrees anticlockwise and the first shape is rotated 90 degrees anticlockwise, the second shape can then be layered over the first shape to give option **b**.
3	d	If the second shape is rotated 180 degrees and the first shape is rotated 90 degrees clockwise, the second shape can be placed below the first shape to give option **d**.
4	c	If the first shape is rotated 90 degrees clockwise, the second shape (if transparent), can be placed directly over the first shape to give option **c**.
5	a	If the second shape is rotated 45 degrees and the first shape is reflected horizontally, the second shape can then be layered over the right side of the first shape to give option **a**.
6	e	If the second shape is rotated 90 degrees clockwise and the first shape is reflected vertically, the second shape can then be layered over the bottom half of the first shape to give option **e**.
7	b	If the second shape is transparent and is rotated 90 degrees clockwise, it can be placed over the top of the first shape. The combined shape can then be rotated 180 degrees to give option **b**.
8	a	If the second shape is transparent and is rotated 90 degrees anticlockwise and the first shape is rotated 180 degrees, the right side of the second shape can then be layered over the left side of the first shape to give option **a**.
9	d	If the second shape is rotated 90 degrees clockwise and the first shape is rotated 180 degrees, the resulting shapes can be layered to give option **d**.
10	c	Layering one shape on top of the other gives option **c**.

Rotation Analogies, pages 49-52

Question	Answer	Explanation
1	b	The first figure in the first pair has been rotated 135 degrees to create the second figure. Therefore, when the first figure in the second pair is rotated 135 degrees, it creates figure **b**.
2	a	The first figure in the first pair has been rotated 200 degrees to create the second figure. Therefore, when the first figure in the second pair is rotated 200 degrees, it creates figure **a**.
3	c	The first figure in the first pair has been rotated 270 degrees to create the second figure. Therefore, when the first figure in the second pair is rotated 270 degrees, it creates figure **c**.
4	b	The first figure in the first pair has been rotated 45 degrees to create the second figure. Therefore, when the first figure in the second pair is rotated 45 degrees, it creates figure **b**.
5	d	The first figure in the first pair has been rotated 60 degrees to create the second figure. Therefore, when the first figure in the second pair is rotated 60 degrees, it creates figure **d**.
6	d	The first figure in the first pair has been rotated 225 degrees to create the second figure. Therefore, when the first figure in the second pair is rotated 225 degrees, it creates figure **d**.
7	d	The first figure in the first pair has been rotated 90 degrees to create the second figure. Therefore, when the first figure in the second pair is rotated 90 degrees, it creates figure **d**.
8	c	The first figure in the first pair has been rotated 180 degrees to create the second figure. Therefore, when the first figure in the second pair is rotated 180 degrees, it creates figure **c**.
9	c	The first figure in the first pair has been rotated 30 degrees to create the second figure. Therefore, when the first figure in the second pair is rotated 30 degrees, it creates figure **c**.
10	d	The first figure in the first pair has been rotated either 180 or 360 degrees to create the second figure. There are no matching options for a 180 degree rotation; option b is close, but the slanting line in the top left circle is slanting in the wrong direction. When the first figure in the second pair is rotated 360 degrees, it creates figure **d**.

© 2018 ElevenPlusExams.co.uk   COPYING STRICTLY PROHIBITED

Reflection Analogies, pages 53-56

Question	Answer	Explanation
1	a	The first figure in the first pair has been reflected in an horizontal mirror line to create the second figure. Therefore, when the first figure in the second pair is reflected in an horizontal mirror line, it creates figure **a**.
2	a	The first figure in the first pair has been reflected in a vertical mirror line to create the second figure. Therefore, when the first figure in the second pair is reflected in a vertical mirror line, it creates figure **a**.
3	c	The first figure in the first pair has been reflected in a vertical mirror line to create the second figure. Therefore, when the first figure in the second pair is reflected in a vertical mirror line, it creates figure **c**.
4	b	The first figure in the first pair has been reflected in an horizontal mirror line to create the second figure. Therefore, when the first figure in the second pair is reflected in an horizontal mirror line, it creates figure **b**.
5	b	The first figure in the first pair has been reflected in a right-leaning diagonal mirror line to create the second figure. Therefore, when the first figure in the second pair is reflected in a right-leaning diagonal mirror line it creates figure **b**.
6	a	The first figure in the first pair has been reflected in a vertical mirror line to create the second figure. Therefore, when the first figure in the second pair is reflected in a vertical mirror line, it creates figure **a**.
7	b	The first figure in the first pair has been reflected in a vertical mirror line to create the second figure. Therefore, when the first figure in the second pair is reflected in a vertical mirror line, it creates figure **b**.
8	d	The first figure in the first pair has been reflected in a right-leaning diagonal mirror line to create the second figure. Therefore, when the first figure in the second pair is reflected in a right-leaning diagonal mirror line it creates figure **d**.
9	a	The first figure in the first pair has been reflected in an horizontal mirror line to create the second figure. Therefore, when the first figure in the second pair is reflected in an horizontal mirror line, it creates figure **a**.
10	d	The first figure in the first pair has been reflected in a right-leaning diagonal mirror line to create the second figure. Therefore, when the second figure in the second pair is reflected in a right-leaning diagonal mirror line it creates figure **d**.

Cross Sections, pages 57-60

Question	Answer	Explanation
1	b	The 3D shape is a cone. As the sliced plane is parallel to the base, the 2D horizontal cross section will be the same as the base, which is a circle. Therefore, the answer is **b**. 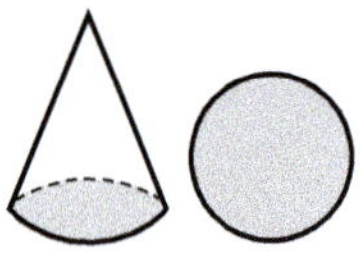
2	c	The 3D shape is a pentagonal prism. As the sliced plane is parallel to the base, the 2D horizontal cross section will be the same as the base, which is a regular pentagon. Therefore, the answer is **c**. 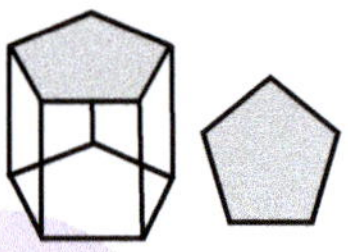
3	e	The diagram on the right shows the 3D shape once the top and bottom cubes have been removed. The shape is made up of two cubes and one long cuboid. As the sliced plane is parallel to the base, the 2D horizontal cross section will be the same as the base, which is a square. Therefore, the answer is **e**. 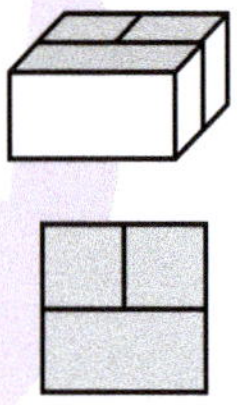
4	d	The 3D shape is a triangular prism with a smaller triangular-prism-shaped hole in the middle. The base of a triangular prism is a rectangle, therefore the 2D horizontal cross section will be a rectangle with a smaller rectangle cut out in the middle. Therefore, the answer is **d**. 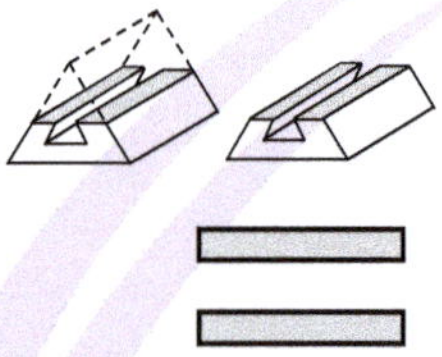
5	a	The 3D shape resembles an hourglass. When sliced through the centre, there will be a plane through the two congruent cylinders and the vertex of both cones. The horizontal cross section of a cylinder is a circle, therefore the 2D horizontal cross section will be two circles with a point in the middle. Therefore, the answer is **a**. 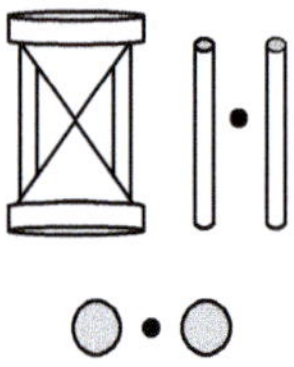
6	d	The 3D shape is a cylinder. The diagrams on the right show how the 2D vertical cross section is formed. Therefore, the answer is **d**. 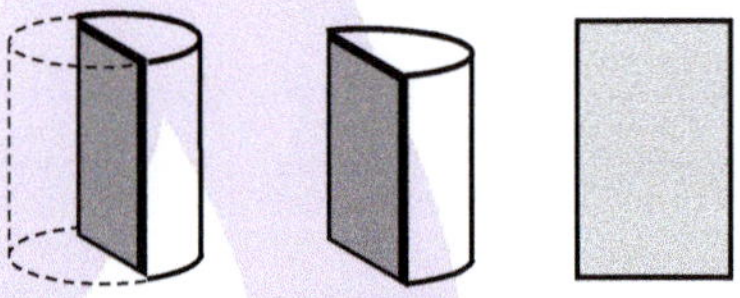
7	b	The 3D shape is an hexagonal prism. As the sliced plane is parallel to the front face, the 2D vertical cross section will be the same as the front face, which is a hexagon. Therefore, the answer is **b**. 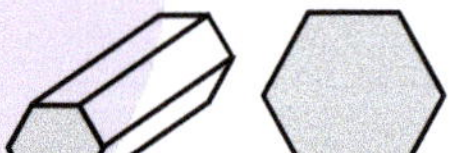
8	d	The 3D shape is a cone. The diagrams on the right show how the 2D vertical cross section is formed. Therefore, the answer is **d**. 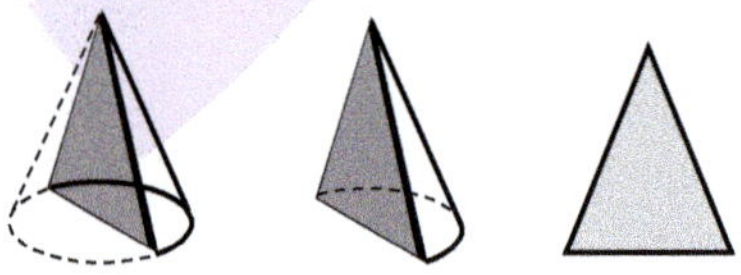
9	d	The 3D shape is a cylinder with a smaller cylinder cut out from the middle. The cross section of a cylinder is a circle, therefore the 2D vertical cross section will be two concentric circles. Therefore, the answer is **d**. 
10	b	The 3D shape is a torus. The 2D vertical cross section through the centre of the torus is two circles. Therefore, the answer is **b**. 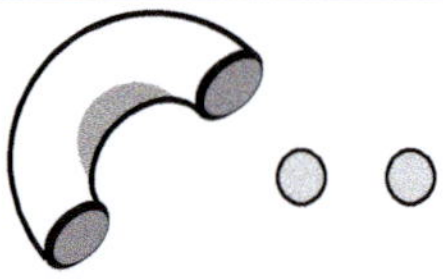

Other Titles in the First Past The Post® Series

Non-Verbal Reasoning: 2D

These books focus on developing the candidate's visuospatial and pattern-identification skills with two-dimensional shapes. Each book provides topic-specific practice, with 15 chapters covering all known question styles likely to come up in 2D Non-Verbal Reasoning 11 plus and Common Entrance exams. Full answers and explanations are included.

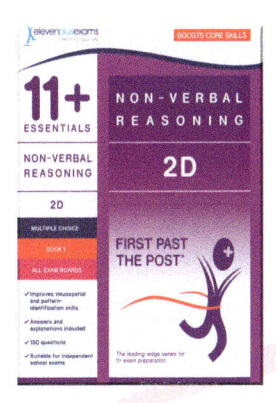

Each book contains 15 topic-specific chapters, each focusing on one of the following: sequences, analogies, codes, similarities, odd one out, complete the square grid, complete the grid, reflections, rotations, hidden shapes, identify the pair, combine the shapes, rotation analogies, reflection analogies and cross sections.

Other Titles in the First Past The Post® Series

Non-Verbal Reasoning: 3D

These books focus on developing the candidate's visuospatial and pattern-identification skills with three-dimensional shapes. Each book contains four topic-specific chapters, each focusing on one of 3D views, 3D composite shapes, 3D cube nets and 3D plan views, and four mixed tests. The mixed tests have been designed to provide real exam practice under a time pressure representative of that in the real exam. Full answers are included.

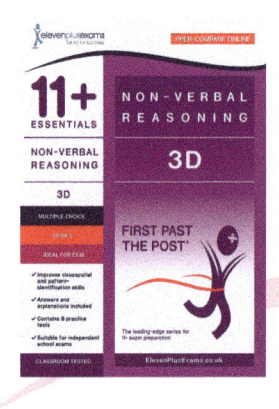

Each test can be marked and evaluated via our Peer-Compare™ Online system, which assesses the candidate's performance anonymously on a question-by-question basis. This helps identify areas for improvement and benchmarks the candidate's score against that of others who have taken the same tests.

Other Titles in the First Past The Post® Series

Non-Verbal Reasoning: Practice Papers (GL)

These books provide real exam practice via four timed tests. These are tailored towards the Granada Learning (GL) Non-Verbal Reasoning assessments but provide invaluable practice for all exam boards. Each test covers a range of 2D question styles, reflecting the likely make-up of the real exam. Full answers and explanations are included.

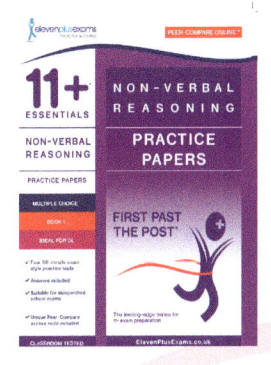

Each test can be marked and evaluated via our Peer-Compare™ Online system, which assesses the candidate's performance anonymously on a question-by-question basis. This helps identify areas for improvement and benchmarks the candidate's score against that of others who have taken the same tests.

Other Titles in the First Past The Post® Series

Verbal Reasoning: Practice Papers (GL)

These books provide real exam practice via four timed tests. These are tailored towards the Granada Learning (GL) Verbal Reasoning assessments but provide invaluable practice for all exam boards. Each test contains a large range of question styles so that, over the four papers, all known questions styles that are likely to come up in the real GL exam are covered. The structure of each test is designed to reflect the likely make-up of the real exam. Full answers and explanations are included.

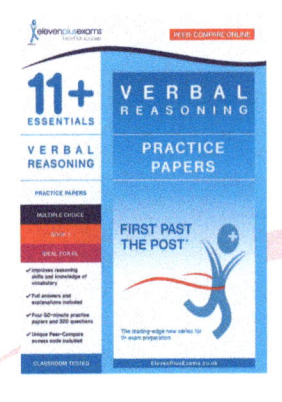

Each test can be marked and evaluated via our Peer-Compare™ Online system, which assesses the candidate's performance anonymously on a question-by-question basis. This helps identify areas for improvement and benchmarks the candidate's score against that of others who have taken the same tests.

Other Titles in the First Past The Post® Series

English: Practice Papers (GL)

These books provide real exam practice via four timed tests. These are tailored towards the Granada Learning (GL) English assessments but provide invaluable practice for all exam boards. Each test comprises a comprehension section and a spelling, punctuation and grammar section, reflecting the likely make-up of the real exam. Full answers and explanations are included.

Each test can be marked and evaluated via our Peer-Compare™ Online system, which assesses the candidate's performance anonymously on a question-by-question basis. This helps identify areas for improvement and benchmarks the candidate's score against that of others who have taken the same tests.

Other Titles in the First Past The Post® Series

Mathematics: Practice Papers (GL)

These books provide real exam practice via four timed tests. These are tailored towards the Granada Learning (GL) Mathematics assessments but provide invaluable practice for all exam boards. Each test covers a large range of topics so that, over the four papers, all known maths topics that are likely to come up in the real GL exam are covered. The structure of each test is designed to reflect the likely make-up of the real exam. Full answers and explanations are included.

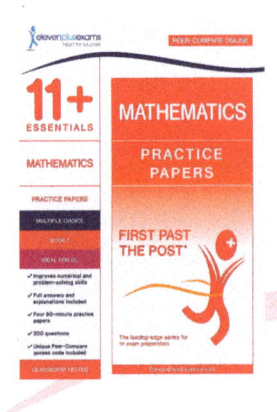

Each test can be marked and evaluated via our Peer-Compare™ Online system, which assesses the candidate's performance anonymously on a question-by-question basis. This helps identify areas for improvement and benchmarks the candidate's score against that of others who have taken the same tests.